MW01601137

Split Decision

SOUTHERLAND | COPYRIGHT 2025

Contents

Chapter 1: The Lifter's Dilemma

The modern gymgoer, armed with more information than ever before, is also more confused. Despite infinite access to routines, splits, influencer programs, and scientific papers, the average lifter struggles to choose a training split that aligns with their body, schedule, and actual goals. The root of this confusion isn't a lack of data—it's a failure of context. Most people aren't making decisions; they're imitating. They follow the routines of influencers with different genetics, schedules, pharmacological support, or training history, and assume the aesthetic result can be traced back to the structure of the split alone. The lifter's dilemma isn't choosing between Upper/Lower, PPL, or Full-Body—it's believing there is a right answer for someone else that automatically becomes the right answer for them.

Historically, splits arose from necessity, not optimization. Bodybuilders in the 1960s trained full-body three times per week because their lives didn't allow otherwise. By the 1980s, drug-assisted athletes moved toward high-volume body-part splits, not because they were better, but because recovery came from syringes. The first misstep was mistaking correlation for causation: beginners assuming six-day bro splits were responsible for Olympia-level physiques, rather than the pharmacological scaffolding and genetic lottery that made those routines survivable in the first place. Today's dilemma is a modern echo of that same confusion—training systems built for specific use-cases are recycled and rebranded as universal solutions.

What social media adds is noise disguised as variety. TikTok compresses a decade of nuanced programming into 15-second montages with zero context. The most viral routines aren't effective—they're cinematic. This breeds a culture of aesthetic mimicry rather than strategic planning. A lifter sees someone with capped delts and striated glutes running a high-frequency PPL split and assumes causality. The result is chronic program-hopping, where each new split is a fresh attempt to replicate someone else's result. This churn rarely improves adherence or outcomes. It merely delays the lifter's ability to assess what's actually working.

The problem compounds when routine choices are driven by fear of missing out. Upper/Lower looks too basic, so it must be inferior. Full-body training feels amateur, so it must be left behind. Push/Pull/Legs offers volume and complexity, so it must be better—until the fatigue sets in. These assumptions are rarely tested; they're adopted wholesale. The real dilemma is that lifters confuse novelty with progress and complexity with superiority. The more advanced the split looks on paper, the more it must be worth, regardless of how poorly it fits their life.

This leads to a quiet, consistent trend across commercial gyms: lifters chasing the ideal split while stuck in a holding pattern. They don't miss workouts out of laziness—they miss them because their split demands more time than they can give. They don't fail to progress due to effort—they fail because their recovery can't keep up with their training volume. They don't quit because the split is wrong—they quit because the split is wrong for them. The dilemma isn't choosing the wrong routine; it's choosing the right one for the wrong reasons.

What's often missing from the conversation is that every split is a compromise. Upper/Lower gives you flexibility and recovery, but it can feel repetitive. Push/Pull/Legs lets you attack volume and isolate muscle groups, but it punishes any break in consistency. Full-body training offers efficiency and simplicity, but it requires intensity and careful exercise selection. No split wins every category. The lifter's dilemma deepens when people try to squeeze a high-volume, high-frequency, isolation-dense split into a schedule that barely fits three gym visits per week. The end result isn't progress—it's program entropy.

Further complicating the issue is the fetishization of athlete routines. Powerlifters run Upper/Lower templates, so recreational lifters adopt them wholesale, ignoring the specificity and accessory work that makes the structure viable. Bodybuilders train six days a week, so amateurs attempt the same without understanding how drugs, genetics, and meal prep sustain that cadence. Olympic lifters train full-body, but under strict supervision and with technique-driven progression that doesn't apply to the average lifter. The dilemma isn't that these templates exist—it's that they're applied blindly, with no audit of individual needs, constraints, or goals.

Even evidence-based communities fall into the same trap. Lifters latch onto meta-analyses and spreadsheet templates without asking whether the data matches their reality. A study might show three full-body sessions outperform bro splits for hypertrophy—but if someone hates full-body training, adherence plummets and results suffer. Another paper might find high-frequency training beneficial for strength—but not if sleep and nutrition are compromised. The lifter's dilemma is thinking evidence provides universal marching orders, rather than inputs for an individualized solution.

The most common consequence isn't injury or overtraining—it's stasis. Lifters spin their wheels under plans they don't understand and can't sustain. They measure results week to week, abandon routines after small plateaus, and redefine "what works" based on YouTube thumbnails. The core misunderstanding is that the split itself isn't magic—it's just a skeleton. Progress depends on how well that structure supports recovery, consistency, and progression. Misaligned splits obscure that fact by making lifters chase features—like frequency or volume—without regard for how they interact with their own training reality.

A useful split is one that disappears into your life, not one that requires a constant reshuffling of it. Yet most lifters design their weeks around training rather than designing their training around their weeks. The illusion of optimization leads to burnout. They schedule a six-day PPL because that's what serious lifters do, then miss sessions every other week and spend the rest of the time in a recovery hole. The split isn't broken—but their relationship to it is.

The answer isn't to retreat into minimalism or renounce structured training. It's to realize that the right split isn't the most complex or popular—it's the one that best supports repeatable execution under the constraints of real life. The lifter's dilemma isn't a matter of science or discipline—it's the disconnect between what a lifter thinks they should do and what they can do consistently, recover from, and adapt to over time.

Until that gap is acknowledged, most lifters will continue to change programs before results have time to materialize. They'll conflate fatigue with effort, variation with progression, and complexity with superiority. They won't fail from lack of effort, but from chasing plans built for other people with other lives. The solution starts not with a new routine, but with rejecting the illusion that someone else's split is the missing variable. The dilemma ends when the lifter stops asking what works best in general and starts asking what works best for them.

Chapter 2: Anatomy of a Split

A training split, at its core, is a logistical decision masquerading as a philosophy. It dictates how training volume is distributed across the week, determining which muscle groups are targeted, how often they are stressed, and how much recovery is allotted between efforts. But the evolution of splits has never been a purely physiological story. It has always been shaped by context: the lifestyle of the trainee, the prevailing dogma of the era, and the silent influence of performance-enhancing drugs. To understand the anatomy of a split is to unravel the assumptions baked into every training schedule—many of which were inherited from athletes with wildly different realities than the average lifter.

The earliest incarnations of structured resistance training, particularly in the first half of the twentieth century, were rooted in full-body routines. Physical culture icons like Reg Park and Steve Reeves built their strength and physique through three-day-per-week training that hit every major muscle group in each session. These workouts were brutal in their simplicity—heavy barbell lifts, minimal isolation, and a limited weekly training frequency dictated as much by life demands as by physiology. Their success reinforced the notion that frequency and compound movement were enough—until drugs and sport-specific training began to rewrite the rules.

By the late 1970s and early 1980s, the bodybuilding landscape shifted. The rise of the Weider system and the steroid-fueled physiques of Olympia competitors brought with them a new template: the body-part split. Monday became chest day, Tuesday back, and so on, with each session laser-focused on a single muscle group, attacking it with high volume and extensive isolation work. This was not the result of a newly discovered hypertrophic principle; it was the result of recovery advantages made possible by exogenous hormones. Muscles could be bombed into oblivion and bounce back within days. The split wasn't scientific—it was pharmacological.

Still, this format spread. Commercial gyms and fitness magazines repackaged it for the masses without modification, ignoring the biological mismatch between elite bodybuilders and natural trainees. The five- or six-day body-part split looked advanced. It offered variety, target specificity, and an air of seriousness. But it also assumed a recovery capacity most people lacked. For decades, this approach dominated mainstream gym culture not because it worked universally, but because it looked like what the winners were doing. The structure was never questioned—it was inherited.

The late 1990s and early 2000s introduced a corrective, largely spurred by strength athletes and coaches who realized the limitations of isolative training. Powerlifters, Olympic lifters, and performance-oriented athletes never abandoned full-body or Upper/Lower structures because those splits aligned better with the demands of movement, frequency, and neurological adaptation. Their approach was never about maximizing the pump—it was about increasing performance across compound lifts, preserving systemic recovery, and progressing across multiple motor patterns weekly. Their splits prioritized skill development and load management over aesthetic isolation.

Out of this tension, the Push/Pull/Legs (PPL) format began gaining traction. It offered a middle ground: more volume and specialization than Upper/Lower, but more frequency and systemic coherence than a bro split. PPL allowed trainees to hit each major muscle group twice weekly if run on a six-day rotation, and it grouped muscles by biomechanical function—pressing, pulling, and lower body—rather than arbitrary anatomical zones. While still popularized through bodybuilding channels, its logic appealed to both hypertrophy enthusiasts and strength-minded lifters seeking more structure than full-body templates but more recovery than body-part isolation provided.

Yet the proliferation of splits—Upper/Lower, PPL, Full-Body, and every hybrid in between—did not resolve the issue. It fractured it. New trainees were no longer following one dominant model; they were inundated with competing frameworks, each claiming superiority. YouTube channels, training apps, and influencer ebooks turned splits into brands. The structure of a training week became a declaration of loyalty rather than a pragmatic decision based on goals, recovery, and constraints. The anatomy of a split became less about muscle group distribution and more about cultural identity within the fitness ecosystem.

Despite the noise, all splits are built on the same three questions: how many days per week can you train, how much volume can you handle and recover from, and how do you want to distribute that work? The answers to those questions should drive the selection, but rarely do. Most lifters pick a split based on what looks hardest, what their favorite physique athlete runs, or what trend is currently circulating in algorithmic loops. They fail to reverse-engineer the structure to their needs. A well-designed split isn't a test of willpower—it's a scaffold for consistent execution.

From a physiological standpoint, there are few hard rules. Muscles do not know what day of the week it is or whether they're part of a Push or Pull session. They respond to mechanical tension, volume, and sufficient recovery. A split simply organizes those factors. It determines how frequently a muscle is stimulated, how much fatigue is carried over between sessions, and how often the nervous system is stressed systemically. In that sense, a split is not a performance driver but a performance container. It holds the variables in place so progression can occur methodically.

For example, an Upper/Lower split might offer two weekly exposures to each major muscle group while alternating between upper and lower body sessions to manage recovery. It works well for lifters training four days per week and seeking balance between hypertrophy and strength. Push/Pull/Legs, on the other hand, front-loads volume and intensity for specific muscle groups in each session but assumes a high training frequency to cycle through all components efficiently. Full-body training concentrates systemic stress into fewer, more comprehensive sessions, making it ideal for time-constrained lifters but demanding higher per-session output and smart exercise rotation to avoid joint strain or excessive fatigue.

Each structure comes with embedded trade-offs. Higher frequency generally improves skill retention and volume distribution but increases the risk of overuse or burnout. Lower frequency allows greater recovery but may require higher per-session intensity to drive adaptation. Specialization allows for targeted growth but can leave systemic qualities— like work capacity or movement proficiency— underdeveloped. The anatomy of a split, then, is less about which muscles are trained when and more about how stress is distributed across time to maximize adaptation without tipping into regression.

Unfortunately, few lifters view splits through that lens. They treat them as set pieces rather than as adjustable frameworks. This leads to rigidity, burnout, or chronic program-hopping. When progress stalls, the instinct is to switch templates rather than evaluate execution or recovery. The irony is that most splits work if applied consistently and adjusted for load, volume, and intensity over time. But that requires understanding the underlying mechanics of a split—not just copying its surface structure.

To dissect a split properly means recognizing it as a system of trade-offs, governed by constraints: time, energy, recovery, and goal specificity. It is not a badge of seriousness or a shortcut to optimization. The anatomy of a split reveals that what matters most is not which format you choose, but how honestly you align it to your life, your physiology, and your capacity to repeat it under stress. When structure supports function—

rather than posturing as a replacement for it—training stops being theoretical and starts being productive.

Chapter 3: Why Upper/Lower Refuses to Die

The continued survival of the Upper/Lower split in a landscape dominated by ever-evolving trends, viral micro-routines, and algorithm-driven programming is less a matter of nostalgia than of stubborn utility. While Push/Pull/Legs and high-frequency full-body approaches cycle through periods of hype, Upper/Lower remains the workhorse quietly producing results behind the scenes. It lacks the novelty that excites beginners and the specialization that flatters advanced trainees, but its enduring relevance stems from the fact that it simply works—predictably, repeatably, and within the time constraints of most real lives. Its refusal to die is not due to cult loyalty but because it answers the central problem most lifters face: how to train hard, recover well, and keep showing up.

At first glance, Upper/Lower appears almost too simplistic. It divides the body into two regions, assigns them alternating training days, and repeats the cycle. This four-day weekly structure—Upper on Monday and Thursday, Lower on Tuesday and Friday—has persisted not because it's flashy but because it naturally balances frequency and recovery. Major muscle groups are trained twice per week, which research consistently shows is an optimal target for hypertrophy in most natural lifters. That frequency avoids the pitfalls of both low-frequency bro splits and the overreach of six-day PPLs, making it sustainable even for those with limited recovery bandwidth or inconsistent sleep, diet, and stress management.

More importantly, the split scales. Unlike rigid templates that assume flawless consistency, Upper/Lower accommodates variability without imploding. Miss one session and the week still holds value. Compress it into three days and nothing breaks. Expand it to five by rotating Upper/Lower/Upper/Lower/Upper and the progression curve holds. The structure has elasticity—a rare trait in program design. This flexibility is what allows it to survive beyond the honeymoon phase of motivation, when the realities of time, fatigue, and adult responsibility begin to exert pressure on even the most well-intentioned training plan.

There's also a biomechanical intelligence embedded in the format, even if it appears on the surface to be unsophisticated. By splitting sessions into upper and lower halves, the body is taxed in alternating systems: upper-body musculature and pressing mechanics one day, posterior chain and squat/deadlift patterns the next. This alternation gives each region at least 48 hours of recovery before its next stimulus, while still maintaining weekly frequency. For natural lifters who lack pharmaceutical recovery support, this balance is non-negotiable. Upper/Lower splits allow for heavy loading, moderate volume, and intensity without constantly tipping into accumulated fatigue or joint stress.

In contrast to body-part splits, which often scatter recovery and overload indiscriminately, the Upper/Lower format clusters fatigue in predictable ways. A heavy squat day may leave the hips, quads, and lower back sore, but those areas aren't needed for the following day's pressing or pulling work. The system naturally avoids overlap, which makes it easier to periodize effectively without constantly bumping into recovery conflicts. PPL, for all its popularity, often blurs those lines—especially when lifters poorly sequence Push and Pull days or front-load the week with maximal volume. Upper/Lower, in comparison, enforces structure that novices and intermediates can execute without deep programming knowledge.

Its continued adoption by strength athletes reinforces this point. Powerlifters, who live and die by their ability to recover between high-effort compound lifts, gravitate toward Upper/Lower splits not because they're trendy but because they're reliable. A typical powerlifting template divides the week into a bench-focused upper day, a squat-focused lower day, a secondary upper session for volume or accessories, and a deadlift-focused lower day. The structure makes logical space for specificity, variation, and fatigue management. It is the same skeleton that beginners adopt, modified through load and exercise selection rather than wholesale reconfiguration. This ability to support both entry-level development and high-level specialization is rare in programming design—and a key reason the format endures.

Upper/Lower also refuses to die because it does not assume perfection. It does not require six days of availability. It does not demand that every body part receive equal psychological attention. It doesn't try to optimize muscle isolation to the point of ignoring systemic fatigue. What it offers is rhythm. Most lifters can anchor to four gym days per week. Most can push hard on a compound lift, back it with assistance work, and still recover in time for the next session. The split doesn't micromanage progression—it gives it room to breathe.

Perhaps most critically, Upper/Lower holds appeal because it doesn't feel dogmatic. Where Push/Pull/Legs often attracts zealots convinced of its superiority, and full-body routines can carry a minimalism-as-virtue narrative, Upper/Lower exists without pretense. It's not advertised as revolutionary or superior. It's not sold as cutting-edge. It simply offers a reliable balance of effort and recovery. That lack of ideological branding allows lifters to inhabit the structure without being seduced by extremes. It accommodates both bodybuilding-style volume and strength-style intensity, provided the lifter knows how to sequence and scale.

Even in hypertrophy-focused circles, where PPL typically dominates, many lifters return to Upper/Lower after burning out. The fatigue cost of six-day training often becomes apparent within two months, especially when paired with demanding lives outside the gym. By contrast, a four-day Upper/Lower split feels attainable and repeatable. Its pacing avoids monotony—alternating training regions ensures variation in movement patterns and physical sensation—while still allowing for enough training density to drive visible change. It's not the most efficient split on paper, but it's the most survivable for the widest range of lifters.

The split's longevity is also reinforced by coaching culture. Many professional strength coaches, particularly in collegiate or private-sector strength and conditioning, rely on variations of Upper/Lower splits to train athletes. The structure allows for predictability, progression, and movement balance across a training week, while avoiding the overlapping fatigue patterns that can interfere with sport-specific performance. When athletes leave that structured environment and continue training recreationally, they often default back to what they know: a simple, effective, four-day system that lets them train hard without breaking down.

Ultimately, the reason Upper/Lower refuses to die is not because it is the best, but because it avoids being the worst at anything that matters. It doesn't require elite recovery or perfect adherence. It doesn't demand six or seven days in the gym. It doesn't overload volume without purpose or scatter fatigue without control. It's not optimized for hypertrophy at the expense of sustainability, nor is it so minimal that progress feels glacial. It occupies the unglamorous center of training design—where real progress happens.

What keeps it alive is not hype or legacy, but function. It works for those who train hard but have lives to manage. It holds up under volume and load, adapts across goals, and survives inconsistency without collapsing. In a fitness world increasingly driven by algorithms, marketing, and aesthetic one-upmanship, Upper/Lower persists because it offers none of those things. It simply delivers results when executed with focus, consistency, and time. That, above all, is why it's still here—and why it's not going anywhere.

Chapter 4: The Logic of Upper/Lower

The logic underpinning the Upper/Lower training split is not theoretical—it is practical. It balances frequency, volume, and recovery in a way that accommodates the body's natural fatigue rhythms while still enabling progressive overload. At its core, the Upper/Lower split divides the body into two major training regions—everything above the waist and everything below—and alternates between them across a weekly cycle. While deceptively simple, this structure maps cleanly onto both biomechanical function and systemic recovery, offering a level of programming clarity that few other splits manage to replicate without additional complexity.

The standard iteration of Upper/Lower is a four-day template. Monday and Thursday are reserved for upper-body sessions, Tuesday and Friday for lower-body work. This sequencing provides roughly 72 hours of recovery between like sessions, assuming a traditional Monday-to-Friday training schedule. That recovery window is not arbitrary. It reflects the general timeline for muscular recovery from moderate to high-intensity resistance training in natural lifters. For trainees pushing compound lifts in each session—bench, overhead press, rows, chin-ups, squats, deadlifts, lunges—this spacing gives just enough time for adaptation without sliding into excessive soreness or neural fatigue that compromises subsequent effort.

One of the central strengths of this split is how cleanly it allows for frequency targets to be met. Most research, including findings published in *Sports Medicine* and *The Journal of Strength and Conditioning Research*, supports the idea that training a muscle group twice per week is superior to once weekly for hypertrophy, particularly in natural lifters not relying on exogenous recovery aids. The Upper/Lower split achieves this frequency without requiring six or seven training days, as Push/Pull/Legs often demands. It offers what hypertrophy-focused templates claim to deliver—adequate volume and frequency—but within a sustainable, four-day structure.

Structurally, the split encourages exercise pairing that respects regional fatigue. In upper-body sessions, pressing and pulling movements can be alternated to allow localized recovery within the workout. A heavy barbell bench press, followed by dumbbell rows or pull-ups, creates natural antagonistic balance. This sequencing prevents systemic overload from clustering in a single motor pattern, something body-part splits routinely mishandle. Instead of bombing the chest with every possible press variation in one session and letting it go dormant for the next seven days, the Upper/Lower split disperses volume across two weekly exposures. This facilitates better movement quality, joint integrity, and cumulative weekly stimulus.

Lower-body sessions follow a similar logic. A Monday squat session does not leave the lifter crippled for the rest of the week because another dose of lower-body training doesn't arrive until Friday. Each leg day can be structured around a dominant movement pattern—knee flexion, hip hinge, or unilateral loading—while still allowing the secondary movement pattern to be addressed without overlap-induced compromise. For example, a Tuesday session may emphasize squats and Bulgarian split squats, while Friday shifts focus to deadlifts and glute ham raises. Each muscle group is trained twice, but through different mechanical emphases, enhancing both hypertrophy and movement economy.

The sequencing also reduces the likelihood of systemic overtraining, especially for intermediate lifters not yet adept at autoregulating effort. Upper and lower sessions draw on different pools of muscular and neural resources, which prevents the accumulation of localized fatigue that occurs in back-to-back Push and Pull sessions, a common flaw in poorly structured PPL routines. By rotating muscle regions, the lifter avoids compounding stress in a way that interferes with both force output and recovery. This rotation is not just about soreness management—it's about preserving high-quality movement across the week.

Another key advantage of the split is its predictability. It doesn't rely on rotating microcycles, floating session structures, or variable intensity weeks to remain viable. The four-day structure becomes a scaffold on which volume, intensity, and load can be periodized cleanly. A lifter can apply linear progression, undulating periodization, or block periodization without needing to reengineer the weekly framework. This makes the Upper/Lower split not just beginner-friendly, but progression-friendly. It simplifies planning while still allowing for complexity in stimulus design.

The split also handles accessory work more gracefully than most realize. Because each session includes multiple major movement patterns—horizontal press, vertical pull, hip hinge, knee flexion—the opportunities for targeted hypertrophy work are evenly distributed. Rather than dedicating an entire session to arms or shoulders, those muscle groups are trained multiple times in support of compound lifts. Triceps are involved in pressing variations twice weekly; biceps are trained through both rows and vertical pulls. This frequency ensures that no muscle group is neglected, and no session is wasted on cosmetic isolation. Accessory work becomes additive, not compensatory.

Where the logic becomes particularly compelling is in its adaptability. A lifter seeking strength emphasis can structure their Upper/Lower split to prioritize heavy compounds early in the week and volume or speed work later. Conversely, a physique-focused trainee can distribute their weekly sets across two sessions per region, using exercise variation to ensure thorough muscle fiber recruitment. The split does not force one training ideology; it accommodates several. It allows intensity, not structure, to dictate focus. That flexibility makes it unusually resilient over long timelines—a quality few other templates can claim.

Unlike Push/Pull/Legs, which often falls apart under inconsistent scheduling, or full-body routines that may suffer from cumulative fatigue if poorly designed, the Upper/Lower split responds gracefully to missed sessions. If a Friday lower-body day is lost, the lifter hasn't gone an entire week without squatting or hinging—they trained legs on Tuesday. This built-in redundancy preserves stimulus density without over-relying on perfect adherence. The logic of the split isn't just about what happens when things go right; it's about how it survives when things don't.

For lifters managing stress, sleep disruption, or erratic schedules, this reliability is more than a convenience—it's a necessity. Program design that assumes perfect conditions will fail as soon as those conditions disappear. The logic of Upper/Lower is that it does not presume anything beyond a reasonable commitment to four weekly sessions and a willingness to train hard. It meets lifters where they are, but still supports progress if they're willing to push effort and control variables.

The elegance of the split lies in its lack of pretense. It makes no claim to be revolutionary, optimized, or individualized. Instead, it offers a mechanical structure that allows lifters to slot in goals, methods, and tools without rearchitecting the schedule. It is not rigid—it is accommodating. Its logic is not theoretical—it is experiential, earned through decades of continued relevance in both physique and performance domains.

Ultimately, the Upper/Lower split persists not because it's perfect, but because it solves the programming puzzle in a way that doesn't require perfect execution. It distributes load and stress rationally, aligns with evidence on frequency and recovery, and supports the full spectrum of training goals—from general strength to targeted hypertrophy. Its logic is not flashy, but it is sound. And in a training culture often dominated by novelty, sound logic remains the most underappreciated asset.

Chapter 5: The Practical Life of Upper/Lower

The real test of any training split isn't how it performs on paper or how it looks in a spreadsheet. It's how it survives real life—late meetings, sick kids, poor sleep, skipped meals, and the thousand unpredictable variables that slowly grind down even the best-laid plans. The Upper/Lower split has earned its longevity not through theoretical superiority, but because it consistently fits the contours of adult life. While many splits ask the trainee to mold their life around the program,

Upper/Lower quietly does the opposite: it adapts to fluctuation without sacrificing effectiveness.

In its standard four-day configuration, the split offers structure without rigidity. The typical Monday–Tuesday and Thursday–Friday setup provides a balanced rhythm of training and rest, creating natural midweek and weekend recovery buffers. For people balancing work, relationships, and fluctuating energy levels, this cadence avoids the burnout associated with six-day splits while still delivering enough training frequency to stimulate progress. If a session is missed, there's no cascading collapse of the week's logic. A skipped Tuesday lower-body day doesn't derail the entire cycle—it gets shifted or absorbed, and the split continues. This resilience is not a side effect—it's the core feature.

For lifters who train after work, the Upper/Lower split also minimizes cognitive friction. Each session has a clearly defined focus. There's no decision fatigue about whether to hit arms or glutes, or whether to squeeze in lateral raises after back extensions. Upper days involve pressing and pulling variations, some direct arm or shoulder work, and maybe a finisher. Lower days center on squats, deadlifts, lunges, or other compound movements, followed by accessories for hamstrings, glutes, and calves. The structure demands intensity, not creativity. This predictability helps lifters maintain consistency in the face of external stressors that would otherwise sap the willpower needed to improvise a coherent session.

The split also maps efficiently onto common weekly energy patterns. Monday tends to be the day of highest compliance—work is structured, motivation is fresh, and fatigue hasn't yet accumulated. Upper-body work fits well here, particularly when it includes heavy pressing or pulling that demands higher neural engagement. Tuesday, slightly diminished in enthusiasm, becomes a lower-body day—a session that may be physically taxing but is less psychologically complex. Wednesday provides a built-in recovery day, intentional or incidental. By Thursday, upper-body work returns without the compounding stress of consecutive lower sessions, and Friday wraps with the week's second leg day. The weekend is then free for rest, mobility, or non-gym activities, without guilt or disruption.

For parents, professionals, or students with non-negotiable time demands, this four-day schedule provides the most training stimulus per time invested. It hits each major muscle group twice per week, leverages compound movements to drive systemic adaptation, and offers sufficient recovery for natural lifters who lack pharmaceutical support. Crucially, it makes no heroic assumptions about available time or perfect adherence. Unlike PPL routines, which unravel quickly if fewer than five sessions are completed per week, Upper/Lower maintains integrity with three. It doesn't punish inconsistency—it absorbs it.

This also makes the split ideal for travel or chaotic schedules. When lifters are pulled into work trips, family events, or social obligations, maintaining a four-day gym rhythm becomes unrealistic. The Upper/Lower format easily compresses or stretches across different timeframes. Three-day variants are simple to execute—rotate sessions sequentially and pick up where you left off. If a lifter only manages two sessions in a week, they've still hit both upper and lower body once. That distribution, while not optimal, still preserves progress and prevents regression. There's no existential crisis about "missing leg day." The structure accounts for disruption without unraveling.

The psychological impact of this cannot be overstated. Many splits fail not due to physical demands, but because they collapse under mental pressure. Lifters who fall behind in a PPL cycle often feel the need to restart, re-sequence, or rebuild the entire week. Full-body routines, while efficient, can feel overwhelming when energy is low—requiring the lifter to push every major muscle group in a single session, even if stress, sleep, or nutrition have been compromised. By contrast, the Upper/Lower split lets lifters focus their limited resources on half the body per session, enabling high-quality work even on suboptimal days.

It also supports more effective autoregulation. When a lifter walks into the gym feeling drained, the reduced session scope makes it easier to adjust volume or intensity without sabotaging the entire plan. A fatigued upper-body day might involve scaling back pressing volume while maintaining pulling intensity. A compromised lower-body day might pivot from heavy squats to moderate RDLs and split squats. Because the split spreads effort across two weekly exposures per region, a downregulated session is just one of two chances to deliver a stimulus—not a catastrophic missed opportunity.

From a recovery standpoint, the format also respects biological limits. Alternating upper and lower body sessions prevents fatigue from clustering in the same muscle groups or movement patterns. This not only supports joint health but also allows connective tissue—often the slowest to adapt— sufficient time to recover between efforts. This is particularly valuable for lifters over thirty, whose training lives must now account for tendon health, sleep variability, and general systemic wear. The built-in spacing of this split keeps recovery honest without demanding aggressive deloading or advanced periodization techniques to stay sustainable.

Even in home-gym settings, where equipment may be limited and session duration is constrained, Upper/Lower remains viable. Upper-body work can be built around push-ups, inverted rows, banded pressing, or dumbbell circuits. Lower-body sessions can be structured with goblet squats, RDLs, lunges, and single-leg movements. The split does not require elaborate machinery or isolation tools to remain effective. Its foundation—compound movement, intelligent sequencing, and weekly frequency—is portable. Lifters moving between gym settings, seasons of life, or levels of motivation can carry the split with them without wholesale redesign.

Coaches and personal trainers also lean into the practicality of Upper/Lower for client programming. It allows for simple progress tracking, clear expectations, and minimal session overlap—ideal when working with busy adults, tactical athletes, or beginners needing structure without overwhelming volume. It also creates natural checkpoints across the week. If soreness is excessive, progression stalls, or sleep suffers, adjusting work in either the upper or lower sessions can restore balance without compromising the entire plan. That modularity gives it a programming advantage in both individualized and group settings.

The appeal, in the end, is not just that it works—but that it keeps working. There is no sharp falloff in effectiveness after the initial novelty fades. There is no strict requirement for high-volume isolation work to maintain balance. There is no dependency on perfect scheduling or elite recovery. The split thrives in the margins—between ideal and acceptable, between perfect execution and sufficient consistency. It holds up not just in lab studies, but in garages, commercial gyms, hotel rooms, and chaotic life schedules.

For lifters seeking a plan that doesn't collapse when life intervenes, the Upper/Lower split remains unmatched. It is not revolutionary. It is not glamorous. It is merely functional in the truest sense of the word—a structure that allows progress to continue in an environment that rarely cooperates. Its strength is not in novelty, but in persistence. It doesn't ask for devotion. It only asks that you show up, four days a week, and train hard. And for most people, that is exactly the kind of program they need.

Chapter 6: Upper/Lower for Hypertrophy

The pursuit of hypertrophy demands consistency, sufficient volume, targeted overload, and recovery that matches output. A split that supports these variables without overcomplicating the weekly structure is rare, which is precisely why the Upper/Lower format remains one of the most viable systems for muscle growth—especially for natural lifters. While it lacks the specialization of bro splits or the brute volume of six-day Push/Pull/Legs routines, the Upper/Lower split excels in one crucial area: it delivers hypertrophy through repeatable, sustainable programming. For lifters willing to trade maximal complexity for long-term progression, it offers an efficient and flexible scaffold for muscle development across all training ages.

At the hypertrophy level, the most advantageous characteristic of the Upper/Lower split is frequency. Hitting each muscle group twice per week sits squarely in the middle of the hypertrophy sweet spot identified in multiple systematic reviews, including the 2016 analysis by Schoenfeld et al., which found that twice-weekly training generally outperforms once-weekly approaches for muscle growth. This frequency allows for more evenly distributed volume without pushing each individual session to failure or into extreme time demands. It also helps maintain quality across sets. Rather than exhausting a muscle with ten variations in one marathon session, the Upper/Lower structure allows lifters to split total weekly work into two focused efforts, enhancing both execution and recovery.

The upper-body sessions can be configured to distribute volume across horizontal and vertical pressing and pulling planes, with accessory work added for deltoids, arms, and scapular stabilizers. This not only supports aesthetic development but also keeps muscle groups like the rear delts, which are frequently neglected in body-part splits, on a consistent stimulus schedule. Similarly, lower-body sessions can alternate between quad- and hip-dominant patterns. One day may emphasize squats and Bulgarian split squats; the other might pivot to deadlifts, RDLs, and glute-focused accessories. This structure enables a form of indirect periodization— variability in exercise selection and emphasis across the week— without needing separate mesocycles.

From a volume standpoint, the Upper/Lower split delivers a realistic ceiling for natural trainees. Evidence suggests that 10–20 sets per muscle group per week can optimize hypertrophy, depending on experience level and recovery. Attempting to cram all 15 sets for chest into a single Monday bro session often leads to diminishing returns—fatigue masks effort, quality drops, and additional sets become junk volume. Upper/Lower distributes that work. Five to eight productive sets for chest on Monday, and another five to eight on Thursday, allow high-quality execution without the psychological burnout or mechanical compromise that creeps into extended sessions. The result is higher output per set, better motor pattern retention, and reduced risk of overuse injuries.

The split also allows for strategic exercise variation. A Monday upper-body session might open with a flat bench press and follow with barbell rows, overhead pressing, and lat pulldowns. Thursday might then rotate to incline pressing, weighted pull-ups, dumbbell shoulder work, and high-rep cable movements. The movement patterns remain consistent, but the angles, loading patterns, and neurological demands vary. This provides enough novelty to prevent stagnation without resorting to unnecessary complexity or abandoning progressive overload. The same applies to lower-body days, where movement rotation can target different fiber types, loading curves, and planes of motion.

Critically, the structure supports systemic recovery—an often-overlooked limiter in hypertrophy programs. When volume is concentrated into six-day splits, the risk isn't just local muscle fatigue, but central fatigue and hormonal suppression, particularly in drug-free lifters. Upper/Lower offers alternating neural demands. After a heavy lower-body day—deadlifts, split squats, or heavy hip thrusts—the following session targets upper-body musculature, giving the posterior chain and CNS an indirect recovery window. This alternation keeps lifters training at high effort without accumulating overlapping fatigue across the week, which is often the hidden cause behind plateaus in aesthetics-driven routines.

For intermediate lifters in particular, this split offers something few hypertrophy templates provide: runway. It scales without imploding. Weekly volume can be increased over time by adding sets across both sessions, not by artificially inflating session length or frequency. Instead of adding another entire training day to accommodate rising demands, a lifter can progress from ten weekly sets per muscle group to fifteen simply by extending work across the existing four-day template. This makes progression feel manageable, both in terms of time commitment and fatigue cost. It also sidesteps the binary thinking common in training culture—the false choice between "going hard" six days a week or being lazy.

Accessory work flourishes under this system. With two upper-body days and two lower-body days, small muscle groups get multiple exposures without dominating the session. Triceps, biceps, and calves don't require full days—they require consistency and sufficient weekly volume. In this format, they receive it as part of a broader, compound-centered session. This embedded frequency is especially useful for developing lagging areas. Rather than throwing a standalone arm day into a five- or six-day split, the Upper/Lower format allows for double stimulus across the week with minimal planning. Rear delts, traps, hamstrings, and even abs can be trained regularly without needing their own spotlight sessions.

The split also lends itself well to progression tracking. Because each major movement has two weekly exposures, feedback is frequent but not excessive. A lifter can measure performance on key lifts—bench, overhead press, squat, deadlift, row—every few days, using the first session for heavy loading and the second for volume or tempo work. This dual exposure supports both mechanical tension and metabolic stress—the two most influential drivers of hypertrophy—without overloading joints or draining motivation. It also gives lifters more chances to auto-regulate based on readiness. If sleep is poor or nutrition suboptimal, volume can be reduced on one day without derailing weekly totals.

Periodization is easy to apply. Within the same structure, blocks of higher volume or higher intensity can be implemented by adjusting rep ranges and rest intervals, not by changing the split. This reduces the programming overhead for lifters without coaching support. There's no need to redesign an entire routine every mesocycle; the framework stays the same while the internal levers shift. That stability supports long-term progression and reduces the tendency to chase novelty for its own sake—an especially common derailment point for intermediate hypertrophy-focused lifters.

Where the split does demand intentionality is in planning balance. Because the Upper/Lower format doesn't handhold isolation work, lazy programming can lead to undertraining certain muscle groups if exercise selection is careless. It's easy to overemphasize pressing over pulling, or squats over hinges. Intelligent lifters must audit their weekly sessions to ensure total muscle coverage. This is not a flaw—it's a feature for those who understand that progression doesn't just come from more work, but from balanced work. When properly designed, the split can match or exceed the effectiveness of more complex routines that disguise volume with unnecessary fluff.

Finally, the psychological pacing of the split is well-suited to hypertrophy's long timeline. Sessions are hard but manageable. Fatigue accumulates but dissipates. Recovery is sufficient, and the format accommodates missed sessions without implosion. Unlike more aggressive routines that burn bright and fade fast, Upper/Lower endures. It rewards consistency, not heroics. And in hypertrophy—where years, not weeks, separate average physiques from remarkable ones—this quality is what separates the lifters who grow from those who simply train.

For those who value muscle growth and have neither the time nor the desire to live in the gym, the Upper/Lower split remains one of the most effective tools available. It is not designed to impress. It is designed to deliver. And for hypertrophy, that distinction makes all the difference.

Chapter 7: Upper/Lower for Strength

For strength-focused lifters, the training split isn't just about organizing muscles—it's about managing fatigue, reinforcing motor patterns, and progressing under load without system failure. The Upper/Lower split has become the backbone of many strength programs for precisely these reasons. Its structure aligns with the demands of neurological adaptation and joint resilience better than nearly any other template. While hypertrophy-oriented lifters can afford to shuffle movements or chase novelty, strength athletes need precision and repeatability. The Upper/Lower split offers both, while still respecting the biological cost of lifting heavy—especially for those not padded by performance-enhancing drugs.

The most valuable aspect of the Upper/Lower split for strength is that it prioritizes compound movement without overloading systemic fatigue. Each session is anchored around one or two high-effort lifts that dominate the neural and muscular demand for the day. In the upper-body sessions, this might mean a heavy bench press or overhead press, followed by rows, chins, and targeted accessory work. For lower-body days, it typically centers around squats or deadlifts, depending on the lifter's goal and programming phase. This structure allows each major lift to have its own platform without overlap. Deadlifting the day after squatting, a common flaw in poorly planned full-body routines, is avoided entirely.

Strength gains depend heavily on frequency, but not in the same way hypertrophy does. The nervous system benefits from regular exposure to heavy loads, but it cannot tolerate chronic overload without compensation. Hitting a lift once a week is often too infrequent to refine technique or stimulate adaptation. Hitting it four times is often unsustainable. The Upper/Lower split, when executed in its classic four-day rhythm, provides a sweet spot—each major lift is trained or closely approximated twice per week, through variations or secondary work, allowing the motor pattern to be reinforced without driving the body into a recovery deficit.

Take, for instance, a lifter prioritizing the big three: squat, bench, and deadlift. Monday's upper-body session might emphasize heavy bench work with back and triceps accessories. Tuesday follows with squats as the primary lift, with hamstring, glute, and quad work layered in to support that pattern. Thursday returns to upper body, potentially with overhead pressing as the main movement and pulling volume to balance pressing frequency. Friday then shifts to deadlift variations, emphasizing posterior chain development and refining hinge mechanics. Over the course of a week, each major lift receives one dedicated session and one supplemental exposure, which keeps the neurological pathways primed without accumulating unsustainable fatigue.

This alternation is a central feature of effective strength programming. The systemically demanding lifts—squats and deadlifts—are spaced apart by 72 hours. Bench pressing and its variations occur with similar spacing, allowing for tissue recovery and nervous system recalibration. This distribution isn't just logical—it's biomechanically protective. Heavy compound lifts stress joints, tendons, and connective tissue far more than hypertrophy-focused isolation work. Without intelligent spacing, these tissues become limiting factors. The Upper/Lower format, by segregating the main lifts and allowing recovery periods between similar movement patterns, enables high-intensity training without incurring breakdown.

Accessory work in strength-focused Upper/Lower templates also benefits from the split's logical separation. Each session has room for targeted volume without intruding on recovery for the next primary lift. On lower-body days, hamstrings, quads, glutes, and core can be trained in support of the main lift without worrying about overlapping with upper-body sessions. On upper-body days, lats, delts, triceps, and biceps can be worked in ways that reinforce the primary pressing or pulling movement without affecting squat or deadlift readiness. This not only supports muscle growth as a secondary benefit but fortifies the muscular and connective support structures needed to prevent injury under load.

Perhaps most important for strength development, the Upper/Lower format allows for coherent progression. Because each primary lift appears at least twice in some form, lifters can apply weekly undulating periodization, alternating heavy and light exposures within the same week. Monday's bench press might be performed at 85–90% of one-rep max for low reps and high intent, while Thursday's session drops the load to 70–75% with higher volume or tempo manipulation. The same applies to squats and deadlifts. This allows volume and intensity to ebb and flow without needing to program entire deload weeks unless fatigue clearly signals the need.

Novice and intermediate strength athletes benefit especially from this frequency and variation. In early stages, motor learning is as important as raw strength adaptation. Repeating movement patterns twice per week accelerates technical proficiency. But unlike full-body programs—which can overload total fatigue when not skillfully adjusted—the Upper/Lower structure preserves session quality. It's not about cramming more lifts into a week; it's about sustaining high performance across fewer, better-structured sessions. This ensures that the lifter's nervous system remains primed, not fried, and that joints stay intact across the long arc of strength development.

Advanced lifters also find value in the split, particularly when combined with microcycle manipulation. A four-day Upper/Lower split allows for focused variations—paused squats, deficit deadlifts, close-grip bench pressing—that target sticking points or weak links without abandoning the basic movement pattern. These variations can be rotated weekly or monthly to address specific technical or muscular deficiencies. Crucially, because the split keeps pressing and lower-body work in separate lanes, each variation can be trained hard without impairing readiness for the next primary session. It supports volume where it's needed and deloads where it's not, a feature often absent in hypertrophy-first programming.

From a programming standpoint, the split lends itself to progressive overload in both linear and non-linear formats. Beginners can ride linear progression with increasing loads across each session, alternating heavier and lighter days as needed. Intermediates might shift to double progression—adding reps or sets within a prescribed load range before increasing intensity. Advanced lifters can program blocks around intensity waves or velocity-based training, using the same four-day structure to manipulate central load markers. None of these systems require a departure from the split itself; the scaffold remains fixed while the internal architecture adapts.

Importantly, the split's time demands are also compatible with strength goals. Four sessions per week provide ample exposure without monopolizing the schedule. Unlike six-day routines, which often assume the lifter has near-professional flexibility, Upper/Lower is realistic. It allows for complete sessions with sufficient rest between efforts, while still offering off days for recovery work, mobility, or simply stepping away from the barbell. That pacing supports the kind of training that's necessary for long-term strength: aggressive, focused, and recoverable.

Some splits collapse under the weight of their own ambition. They ask too much of the lifter, demand too many days, or scatter fatigue across sessions until quality vanishes. The Upper/Lower split avoids that trap. It keeps the priorities clear: one region per session, one major lift per day, one goal per week—get stronger. And it does this not by minimizing work, but by managing it. That distinction is what makes it one of the most effective, resilient, and coachable structures for strength development—regardless of training age or end goal.

In the long game of strength, where each additional five pounds lifted represents hours of cumulative work, efficiency matters as much as effort. The Upper/Lower split offers both. It doesn't romanticize complexity. It doesn't bury lifters under volume for its own sake. It simply provides the right amount of exposure, the right distribution of stress, and the right rhythm of recovery—week after week, cycle after cycle. And for those serious about getting stronger without compromising longevity, that rhythm is everything.

Chapter 8: The Science Behind PPL Worship

The reverence surrounding the Push/Pull/Legs split—often abbreviated as PPL—rests on a combination of surface logic, cultural momentum, and a selective reading of training science.

For a generation of lifters steeped in Reddit threads, YouTube thumbnails, and Instagram influencers flexing beneath overhead gym lights, PPL appears as the apex of training design. It promises volume, frequency, specialization, and modularity in a format that feels both advanced and intuitive. But its appeal isn't purely aesthetic. At its core, PPL is a mechanical structure that aligns reasonably well with established hypertrophy principles, particularly when executed with discipline and precision. The science behind its popularity isn't imagined—but it is often misapplied, misunderstood, or distorted by overreach.

At the most basic level, PPL divides the body into three mechanical functions: pushing (horizontal and vertical presses), pulling (rows, pull-ups, curls), and lower-body movements (squats, hinges, and leg-specific accessories). This structure mirrors the way compound lifts naturally organize themselves, making session planning feel organic rather than forced. The separation of muscle actions minimizes overlap, reducing the likelihood of cumulative fatigue across sessions. Unlike body-part splits, where pressing may reappear every other day under a different name—chest on Monday, shoulders on Wednesday, triceps on Friday—PPL clearly groups synergistic muscles and gives them focused attention with full recovery windows in between.

This logical separation supports the implementation of higher training frequency. When PPL is run in a six-day rotation—Push, Pull, Legs, rest, repeat—each muscle group is hit approximately twice per week. That frequency matches what hypertrophy-focused literature consistently identifies as optimal for natural lifters. A 2018 review in *Frontiers in*

Physiology underscored that stimulating a muscle group every 48 to 72 hours appears ideal for maximizing protein synthesis and muscle growth without surpassing recovery thresholds. PPL aligns with that frequency—at least in theory—while providing enough intra-session volume to accumulate a meaningful growth stimulus across multiple angles and rep ranges.

Volume is the second reason PPL has captured the loyalty of high-frequency trainees. The structure naturally encourages 15 to 20 sets per major muscle group per week when executed in full. That target lands squarely within the hypertrophic volume guidelines put forth by studies such as those by Brad Schoenfeld and James Krieger, which argue that advanced trainees often benefit from higher weekly set counts, provided recovery and intensity are controlled. Because PPL splits muscles across three categories instead of body-part isolation, they allow for more exercise variety and volume distribution without bloated, three-hour training sessions. A Push day might include incline presses, overhead work, dips, and lateral raises, each contributing to a muscle group's total weekly load without needing to annihilate it in a single session.

The split also supports progressive overload through repeat exposures. Hitting the same muscle groups twice weekly allows for both a primary heavy session and a secondary volume-focused or variation-based session. This frequency permits technical refinement, accommodates multiple rep ranges, and enables more complex periodization models to flourish. Lifters can rotate rep schemes, manipulate rest periods, or implement advanced methods—rest-pause, myo-reps, tempo work— within a stable structure that repeats every three days. The continuity allows fatigue to be tracked and managed more precisely than once-a-week splits, where fluctuations in performance are often masked by the long gaps between exposures.

Perhaps the most underrated aspect of PPL is its modularity. Unlike full-body or Upper/Lower splits, which typically presume four or three weekly sessions, PPL can be tailored to virtually any training frequency. On a three-day schedule, the lifter performs one Push, one Pull, and one Legs session per week. On a four-day schedule, they rotate through the sessions continuously, picking up where they left off. On a six-day schedule, each movement pattern is trained twice, maintaining optimal frequency for hypertrophy. This adaptability makes PPL attractive to a wide range of lifters who want structure but cannot guarantee the same number of training days every week.

The structure also lends itself well to perceived autonomy, which is often conflated with customization. Lifters can fill their Push day with incline dumbbell presses, barbell overhead presses, and cable flyes—or swap in machine work or dips based on their preferences, equipment availability, or joint health. Pull days can be built around chin-ups and rows, or high-rep lat pulldowns and biceps supersets. This variability creates a sense of ownership and control over training, even if the underlying principles remain consistent. It feels advanced, but also personal, which contributes to its widespread adoption across social media platforms where uniqueness is often mistaken for expertise.

Cultural reinforcement plays a role here as well. PPL has become a social signal among self-identified serious lifters. It sits in contrast to full-body training, which is often associated—incorrectly—with beginners, or body-part splits, which are linked to outdated bodybuilding dogma. PPL is marketed as the evidence-based alternative, even when applied haphazardly. Influencers display their six-day PPL routines as a badge of volume tolerance, intensity, and discipline. The split becomes more than a system—it becomes a standard, one that implicitly suggests that training anything less than six days per week is a concession to mediocrity. The science supports PPL when properly executed, but the culture surrounding it often exaggerates its superiority.

This is where the gap between evidence and execution emerges. While the framework of PPL aligns with hypertrophy literature in terms of frequency, volume, and exercise variation, its effectiveness depends entirely on programming quality and recovery management. Most lifters, seduced by the promise of rapid gains, treat PPL as a six-day race to nowhere—stacking maximal volume into each session without accounting for intensity, load progression, or fatigue. The science behind the split offers principles; the culture around it often ignores nuance in favor of maximalism.

When used intelligently, however, PPL can serve as a legitimate hypertrophy vehicle. Its structure allows for refined movement pattern balance, regular technical rehearsal, and systematic volume loading across all major muscle groups. The separation of muscle groups by function—not just anatomy—encourages comprehensive training. Pressing, pulling, and lower-body efforts each receive their own spotlight, and within those sessions, multiple movement types can be explored. Horizontal and vertical planes, compound and isolation lifts, free weights and machines—all can coexist in a rotation that minimizes redundancy and promotes adaptation.

For natural lifters with the time, motivation, and recovery capacity to train five or six days per week, PPL is a scalable and scientifically sound option. Its architecture provides the framework, but the outcome hinges on execution. Without controlled effort, load progression, deload phases, and recovery hygiene, the split becomes a high-frequency dead end—one that looks impressive on paper and online but stalls in practice.

The science behind PPL worship is real, but partial. It aligns with hypertrophy research when structured well, but it's not inherently superior to other formats like Upper/Lower or Full-Body. Its success depends not on how often it's done, but on how intelligently it's run. Volume and frequency are tools, not virtues. When that distinction is understood, PPL becomes what it should be: a structured way to grow, not a cult to belong to.

Chapter 9: Structuring a Real PPL Week

The popularity of the Push/Pull/Legs split has led to widespread adoption, but also widespread misapplication. While its structure appears straightforward—train pushing muscles one day, pulling muscles the next, legs on the third—it's rarely executed with the level of precision required to make it sustainable, productive, and recovery-balanced. The version that floods fitness forums and influencer posts is usually a caricature: a six-day grind with maximal volume, minimal rest, and no understanding of fatigue management. To structure a real PPL week—the kind that produces long-term hypertrophy without burying the lifter in chronic soreness or neural exhaustion—requires more than just assigning muscles to days. It demands a nuanced understanding of sequencing, frequency, and adaptive volume control.

A functional PPL week begins with an honest inventory of how many training days are available. The textbook PPL template is six days: Push, Pull, Legs, repeat. This cycle allows each major muscle group to be trained twice per week, a frequency supported by literature as effective for maximizing hypertrophy. But the fatal flaw is assuming six-day consistency is sustainable. Most lifters cannot reliably train six consecutive days without a collapse in execution, intensity, or recovery. The structure is viable only if the quality of effort remains high, sleep and nutrition are tightly managed, and stress outside the gym is low. This scenario fits a tiny minority of trainees—typically younger, genetically resilient, and free from adult responsibilities. For everyone else, a more intelligent structure is required.

A four- or five-day variant offers a more practical rhythm. In a four-day schedule, the PPL sequence becomes continuous rather than calendar-fixed: the lifter trains Push on Monday, Pull on Wednesday, Legs on Friday, and the fourth session (Push again) on Saturday or Sunday. The following week picks up with Pull, then Legs, and so on. Over a two-week cycle, each muscle group still receives roughly three sessions, preserving hypertrophy frequency while allowing rest days to be dictated by real life rather than spreadsheet perfection. This rotating schedule avoids burnout while maintaining forward progression—a crucial adjustment most lifters overlook.

Even with six training days available, sequencing matters. Poorly structured PPL weeks often fail by stacking neural and joint stress too aggressively. For instance, starting the week with a maximal-effort Push session—heavy bench, overhead pressing, weighted dips—can leave the shoulders, triceps, and upper back under-recovered for the very next Pull day. Overlap isn't just theoretical; pressing and pulling rely on shared joint structures and stabilizers. A smarter sequencing approach staggers loading. If Monday's Push session emphasizes horizontal pressing and shoulder work, Tuesday's Pull session should pivot to vertical pulls and machine-based rows to reduce joint strain. Similarly, if Wednesday's Legs session includes high bar squats and lunges, Thursday's Push session should be lighter, or even reserved for accessory work, rather than immediately jumping into overhead barbell pressing.

A more sophisticated version of the PPL split alternates between heavy and moderate days for each muscle group. For example, the first Push session might prioritize heavy compounds—barbell bench press and strict overhead press—while the second uses dumbbells, cables, and higher rep ranges to reduce axial loading. Pull sessions can follow the same logic: one built around heavy rows and weighted pull-ups, the other emphasizing lat pulldowns, machine rows, and rear delt isolation. This intra-week variation not only spreads volume more evenly, it also modulates fatigue, allowing muscle groups to be trained frequently without entering recovery debt. Strength-focused variations can alternate rep ranges more dramatically, while hypertrophy-focused lifters may simply shift from 6–10 reps early in the week to 12–15 later.

Lower-body sessions present their own challenges. Legs are neurally demanding, systemically fatiguing, and often neglected in favor of upper-body volume. A poorly planned PPL week places them mid-week, surrounded by aggressive upper-body work that saps energy and reduces focus. A better model treats leg sessions as tent poles—either bookending the week (Monday and Friday) or splitting the week in half with full recovery on either side. One session might prioritize knee-dominant work—front squats, split squats, leg extensions—while the second leans into hip-dominant patterns like RDLs, glute bridges, and hamstring curls. This alternation maintains balance, avoids pattern redundancy, and improves long-term adherence for lifters who dread leg training.

Recovery days need to be strategically placed. A real PPL week should never go six days straight unless volume is capped, intensity is modulated, and sleep is dialed in. A more effective layout is a 3-on, 1-off structure: Push, Pull, Legs, rest, then repeat. This allows recovery to accumulate while keeping weekly frequency high. It also creates a psychological checkpoint—day four becomes a reset rather than a collapse. If the lifter hits Monday through Wednesday hard, Thursday becomes a controlled pause, preventing the tail end of the week from becoming an exercise in survival. The result is not fewer sessions—it's better sessions, sustained over longer cycles.

Within each session, volume must be tailored based on the number of exposures that week. In a six-day plan, each session carries less volume—typically 10–12 sets across all exercises—because total weekly exposure is high. In a four-day plan, that number climbs to 14–16 per session to compensate for reduced frequency. The mistake most lifters make is applying six-day session volume to four-day frequency, producing sessions that exceed two hours and create more fatigue than adaptation. Progress stalls not because the split is flawed, but because volume is misaligned to frequency.

Session construction should also reflect movement balance. A Push session isn't just about chest—it must include horizontal and vertical presses, lateral delts, and triceps, ideally with both compound and isolation work. A Pull session isn't just for lats—it must include horizontal rows, rear delts, biceps, and scapular stabilizers. A Legs day isn't complete with squats alone—it requires hip hinges, unilateral work, and calf training. Real PPL programming covers all these planes of motion, often with a rotation of exercise selections across the week to prevent overuse and promote joint health.

Fatigue monitoring is another critical layer. In high-frequency PPL setups, performance should be assessed session to session—not just for load progression, but for movement quality, bar speed, and joint feedback. If sleep, stress, or nutrition falter, intensity and volume must be adjusted mid-week. The benefit of PPL is frequency; the risk is overconfidence in that frequency. A lifter who ignores these signs will plateau quickly or regress, not because the structure is broken, but because it was applied with blind rigidity.

Real PPL programming respects that lifters live in real conditions—job deadlines, sleep disruption, emotional fatigue. The split must flex with those variables. Training six days per week is not a badge of discipline; it's a demand on the recovery system. Structured correctly, a PPL week delivers consistent hypertrophy stimulus with modular volume, movement variety, and a fatigue pattern that a natural lifter can survive and progress under. Structured poorly, it becomes a high-frequency cul-de-sac that leads only to burnout and stagnation.

The beauty of PPL lies not in its surface simplicity, but in how much adaptability it offers beneath that surface. A real PPL week isn't about stacking workouts—it's about sequencing stress, modulating volume, and rotating emphasis with enough precision to grow without breaking. When those elements are aligned, PPL ceases to be a trend and becomes what it should be: a rational, resilient template for long-term progress.

Chapter 10: PPL in the Wild

In theory, the Push/Pull/Legs split is a marvel of symmetry and efficiency. In practice, it often collapses under the weight of real life. The structured elegance of Push one day, Pull the next, Legs to follow, repeated in a six-day loop, assumes a level of scheduling precision, recovery capacity, and motivational consistency that most lifters simply don't possess. Once removed from the realm of spreadsheets and Instagram graphics, PPL begins to reveal its cracks—not because the structure is flawed, but because it is often imposed without considering the constraints that shape real-world training: time, energy, unpredictability, and the simple fact that people don't live like algorithms.

The typical application of PPL in commercial gyms tells the story. A lifter commits to six sessions a week, often inspired by a shredded influencer or a popular eBook promising high-frequency hypertrophy. The first week goes well—Push on

Monday, Pull on Tuesday, Legs on Wednesday, repeated again Thursday through Saturday. But by week two, cracks form. A late work meeting on Wednesday forces the leg day to be skipped. Now, the lifter debates whether to shift the week, repeat Push, or double up later. By week three, a social event, poor sleep, or illness disrupts the sequence again. The lifter now faces a fractured rotation, confusion about recovery timing, and frustration about lost momentum. What started as a well-intentioned plan devolves into improvisation.

This fragility stems from a rigid dependency on continuity. Unlike Upper/Lower or Full-Body templates, which remain stable even when condensed to three sessions, PPL loses coherence when consistency falters. If a lifter misses one session in a six-day PPL plan, an entire region goes untrained for over a week. Missing a Pull session doesn't just delay biceps and lats—it throws off recovery balance, progression schedules, and accessory pairing. The result is often either compensation through poor-quality catch-up sessions or outright abandonment of the cycle in favor of something "more manageable." In the wild, the very frequency that makes PPL look optimal often becomes its undoing.

Another issue that emerges in real-world application is volume drift. Most lifters, aiming to make each session "worth it," tend to overprogram individual days. Push sessions swell with flat bench, incline dumbbells, overhead barbell press, dips, and lateral raises. Pull days stack rows, pull-ups, pulldowns, face pulls, curls, and shrugs. Legs days become an ordeal of squats, lunges, leg press, hamstring curls, RDLs, and calf work. Sessions stretch past 90 minutes, not because of necessity, but because the frequency target creates a false sense of urgency to hit everything, every time. In reality, the program becomes overloaded and unsustainable, increasing systemic fatigue while eroding recovery margins between days.

Recovery, in fact, is where PPL often quietly fails for natural trainees. In high-frequency use, it assumes not just consistent energy availability, but also adequate sleep, nutrition, and stress management—all of which are unpredictable in non-athletic life. Heavy pressing on Monday taxes shoulders, elbows, and the upper back. Pulling on Tuesday loads the spine and rear delts. By Wednesday, a leg session feels less like a new stimulus and more like a last-man-standing challenge. That fatigue doesn't reset with sleep—it accumulates. Without pharmacological support or lifestyle insulation, most lifters gradually under-recover, misattribute it to stagnation, and begin cycling through variations in search of a solution that isn't structural—it's practical.

This fatigue pattern also plays out neurologically. PPL often fails to account for the overlapping neural demands of consecutive heavy compound lifts. A heavy Push day might involve barbell bench and overhead press—two lifts requiring high motor unit recruitment and trunk stabilization. Pull day follows with heavy barbell rows and weighted pull-ups, which again challenge posture, grip, and spinal loading. Legs on day three brings squats and hinges, which impose the heaviest systemic stress of the week. Across these three days, the nervous system is taxed without reprieve. Even if different muscles are being trained, the same core structures—spinal erectors, hips, shoulders—are repeatedly stressed, leaving the lifter neurologically drained by mid-week, even if no single session feels excessive.

51

When lifters begin to flag, the temptation is to reduce rest between sets or decrease load to preserve schedule fidelity. But this only masks the issue. Without sufficient recovery between sessions, movement quality degrades, joint stress compounds, and the overall training signal weakens. What began as a high-frequency hypertrophy plan becomes a repetitive circuit of moderate-effort sessions that feel productive but fail to stimulate meaningful growth or strength. In real-world terms, this is where lifters stall: still training six days a week, still sweating, still moving weight—but adapting less and feeling worse.

Another common problem with PPL in practice is psychological fatigue. Repeating the same three-day cycle ad nauseam can lead to monotony, especially if exercise selection remains static. Push day begins to feel indistinguishable from the one before it, as do Pull and Legs. Without strategic variation or intelligent rotation, motivation wanes. Some lifters attempt to solve this by changing exercises weekly, but this only dilutes progression tracking and undermines overload. Others swap rep schemes randomly, further derailing consistency. The structure becomes a holding pattern rather than a growth engine—predictable, repetitive, and ultimately dull.

There's also the reality of life's asymmetry. Most people don't distribute their energy evenly across the week. Monday workouts benefit from weekend rest. By Thursday or Friday, accumulated work stress, social obligations, or mental fatigue reduce output. In a rigid six-day PPL cycle, the quality of each session depends heavily on external factors the split doesn't account for. The assumption that every session can be executed with similar intensity, attention, and recovery is theoretical at best, delusional at worst. The best-case scenario—a perfectly recovered, high-effort week—is the exception, not the rule. In the wild, it rarely materializes beyond the first few weeks of a new program.

Yet despite these failings, PPL remains popular because when done well, it does work. It provides targeted stimulus, allows for volume accumulation, and encourages frequency—all beneficial for hypertrophy. But in order for it to succeed outside the lab or the lens of social media, it must be adapted. Training six days per week must be treated as an option, not a requirement. Fatigue must be monitored across the week, not ignored in favor of schedule purity. Rest days should be placed deliberately, not just squeezed in when exhaustion becomes impossible to ignore. And volume must be distributed intelligently—not stacked blindly for the sake of hitting a muscle twice.

Real-world PPL isn't glamorous. It's slower, messier, and more adaptive than the fantasy versions. It means sometimes running a five-day cycle over eight or nine days. It means trimming volume on Pull day because Push went too hard. It means substituting barbell rows for machines when grip is fried. It means skipping a session, then calmly resuming the rotation rather than panicking and restarting. The difference between success and stagnation is not the split itself—it's how well it survives under pressure.

Push/Pull/Legs, in the wild, must shed its perfectionism to be useful. It must be flexible without becoming random, disciplined without becoming rigid. When lifters stop treating the split as gospel and start treating it as a framework—an adaptable system built around effort, not dogma—it becomes what it always promised to be: a highly effective structure for training hard, often, and intelligently. But only when the real world is allowed into the plan.

Chapter 11: PPL for Mass and Volume

The Push/Pull/Legs split is practically engineered for volume. Its design, when correctly applied, allows lifters to accumulate a high workload across all major muscle groups without overstuffing any single session with excessive fatigue or mechanical overlap. For hypertrophy—especially in the intermediate to advanced range—the capacity to apply sustained, targeted volume over time is one of the most reliable predictors of muscular growth. PPL thrives in this environment because it doesn't just tolerate volume; it organizes it with precision. When executed intelligently, the split allows for both muscle-specific overload and systemic recoverability, making it one of the most scalable frameworks for mass-focused training.

The appeal begins with the split's frequency: a six-day cycle allows each movement pattern—and thus each major muscle group—to be trained twice per week. Unlike body-part splits that often operate on a once-weekly cadence, PPL enables the distributed exposure necessary to maintain high-quality volume without overreaching in a single session. For hypertrophy, this matters. Studies, including Schoenfeld's 2016 meta-analysis, show that training a muscle group twice weekly consistently outperforms once-weekly routines for mass, especially in drug-free lifters. PPL offers this twice-per-week exposure by design, without requiring compromise on intensity or exercise variety.

The structure of the split allows each session to focus narrowly, which enhances volume quality. On a Push day, for example, all pressing and shoulder work can be programmed without interference from posterior-chain fatigue or lower-body strain. The nervous system and joints are not splitting attention across multiple planes or regions. This concentrated workload improves mind-muscle connection, preserves movement pattern integrity, and permits more refined exercise selection. A session might include incline barbell press, overhead dumbbell press, weighted dips, lateral raises, and triceps work—all targeting distinct areas of the push musculature. The result is dense volume directed with intent, not just effort.

Pull days follow suit. Horizontal rows, vertical pulls, rear delt work, biceps curls, and scapular stability drills all live under the same roof. With no pressing to compete with, these muscles receive unshared attention and loading. It allows lifters to chase meaningful volume in back and biceps without the fatigue leakage common in full-body or Upper/Lower splits, where grip and spinal fatigue often accumulate earlier in the week. The psychological pacing is also smoother. When lifters know the entire session is devoted to pulling mechanics, they can focus effort and time accordingly, rather than rushing through accessories to make space for unrelated muscle groups.

Leg days, while often underappreciated, are where the PPL structure reveals its hypertrophy engine. Devoting an entire session to lower-body work without upper-body interference allows for more comprehensive programming. Compound lifts—squats, lunges, RDLs, leg presses—can be followed by isolation work for quads, hamstrings, and calves without racing the clock. This focused structure reduces the common trade-off between doing squats well and neglecting glute or hamstring volume. Instead of seeing legs as a single lift followed by token effort, PPL leg sessions are platforms for full-spectrum lower-body training—an approach often neglected in higher-frequency full-body programs where leg work is trimmed to make room for upper-body staples.

One of the core advantages of the PPL split for mass is how cleanly it separates overlapping muscle groups across the week. In a Push day, the triceps are hit indirectly through presses and directly through extensions. They receive 48 to 72 hours of recovery before being taxed again on Pull or Legs days, where they play little to no role. Similarly, back and biceps get their own window of stimulus without interference. This clean division of effort allows for a high total weekly set count without stacking fatigue in the same joints or tendons day after day—a problem common in poorly organized bro splits or minimalist full-body routines.

When programmed for hypertrophy, each session typically includes three to four compound or multi-joint exercises and two to three isolation movements, totaling 15 to 20 working sets per session. Across six sessions, this generates 90 to 120 sets per week—a volume level well-suited for advanced lifters with recovery capacity to match. That range exceeds the threshold for minimum effective volume while staying below the ceiling where junk volume accumulates and recovery suffers. The structure allows progression through double progression models, incremental load increases, or rep cycling—all of which are easier to implement when the same muscles are trained twice per week.

That said, volume in PPL must be managed—not indulged. The temptation in a hypertrophy context is to view each session as an opportunity to destroy the muscle group, especially since the same muscles won't be trained again for two or three days. This approach backfires quickly. Overreaching in early sessions leads to underperformance in later ones. A real mass-building PPL program distributes volume strategically: one Push session might carry heavier pressing and moderate accessory work, while the second leans into higher reps, machines, and lighter isolation. This rotation allows for cumulative volume without overloading joints or undercutting recovery.

Similarly, Pull days can be alternated. One session might emphasize horizontal pulling with moderate intensity, while the other emphasizes vertical pulling and higher rep ranges. Leg days can be split between quad-dominant and posterior-chain-dominant emphases, reducing redundant loading and allowing muscles to recover differentially across the week. This intra-week variation is key. It prevents boredom, reduces injury risk, and maintains volume quality across long hypertrophy phases.

Recovery also demands active management. Sleep, nutrition, and rest-day scheduling are not optional luxuries—they're non-negotiable variables in a high-volume PPL plan. Without proper recovery infrastructure, the split's greatest asset—frequency—becomes its greatest liability. The same lifter who thrives on six PPL sessions during a deloaded work schedule might find themselves crushed by the same structure during periods of stress or poor sleep. When recovery falters, the solution isn't necessarily fewer sets per session but smarter session sequencing and volume scaling across the week.

Psychological fatigue must also be addressed. High-frequency training requires mental buy-in and program variety to remain sustainable. A PPL plan focused purely on mechanical execution, with no rotation in rep schemes or exercise selection, quickly turns stale. Periodizing rep ranges—cycling between strength-focused (6–8), hypertrophy-focused (8–12), and endurance-based (12–15) blocks—not only drives adaptation but keeps engagement high. The same can be done with equipment: barbell, dumbbell, machine, cable. These shifts maintain novelty while preserving structure—a crucial balance for long-term adherence.

Ultimately, PPL is one of the few splits that allows lifters to chase volume with purpose. It provides a platform for high-effort work without compromising mechanical balance, movement diversity, or recovery bandwidth—if programmed correctly. It creates space for the type of consistent, high-quality output that builds muscle not in weeks, but in years. For intermediate and advanced lifters with the discipline to manage fatigue and the patience to periodize their effort, PPL offers the clearest path to long-term hypertrophy.

What PPL does not do is make that growth automatic. Volume without control is just exhaustion. Frequency without strategy is just noise. But when volume, frequency, and structure are aligned, PPL becomes more than a training split—it becomes a hypertrophy system. And when executed with precision, it delivers what most lifters claim to want: sustained, measurable, muscular growth. Not as a promise, but as a process.

Chapter 12: PPL for Strength Gains

The Push/Pull/Legs split is rarely the first recommendation for strength development, and not without reason. It was designed around hypertrophy—volume accumulation, muscular balance, and high-frequency exposure—not maximal neural efficiency. Yet many lifters attempt to repurpose it for strength, hoping that the structure that builds mass can be twisted, with minimal adjustment, into a system that also builds load capacity. The truth is more nuanced. While PPL isn't inherently optimized for strength, it can be made to serve that goal—provided the lifter makes deliberate modifications, resists the urge to chase volume for its own sake, and retools the split to respect the unique recovery demands of heavy lifting.

The primary limitation of PPL for strength is its lack of systemic fatigue management. Strength adaptations, unlike hypertrophy, are central nervous system–dependent. They rely on maximal or near-maximal loads, low-rep sets, and high inter-set rest. This training style imposes significant neural stress, especially when performed across multiple days with minimal recovery between sessions. A standard six-day PPL—Push, Pull, Legs, repeated—simply does not allow adequate time for this type of recovery to occur. Attempting to squat on Wednesday after heavy benching Monday and deadlifting Tuesday is a predictable path to underperformance, technical breakdown, or stalled progression.

To make PPL viable for strength, the structure must first be decelerated. Three or four training days per week—not six—becomes the starting point. This shift sacrifices frequency in favor of output quality. One possible format is a rotating PPL over four days: Week one includes Push, Pull, Legs, Push; week two begins with Pull, Legs, and so on. This slower cycle preserves muscle group exposure while creating recovery windows long enough to accommodate heavy loading. It also prevents the most common PPL mistake: attempting to layer strength programming on top of hypertrophy-level volume, then wondering why progress stalls after six weeks.

Once frequency is reduced, session structure must follow suit. Strength-focused sessions do not require ten exercises and seventy total working sets per week. They require three to five lifts per day, each executed with high intent, long rest intervals, and tight technical control. A strength-based Push day, for example, might include barbell bench press (5x3 at 85–90% 1RM), incline dumbbell press (3x8 at moderate RPE), and a triceps accessory movement (3x10). That's it. More would compromise recovery. Similarly, a Pull session might focus on weighted pull-ups or barbell rows for low reps, followed by direct biceps or rear delt work to maintain joint balance and musculature without introducing excessive fatigue.

Leg sessions, the most taxing of the three, demand particular restraint. Squats and deadlifts—whether trained together or separately—must be programmed with clear intention. Attempting to go heavy on both in the same session, then repeat that effort three days later, is incompatible with recovery timelines for strength development. One solution is to alternate emphases weekly: week one prioritizes squats; week two, deadlifts. The secondary lift is still present but performed at lower intensity or with a variation—paused squats, Romanian deadlifts, front squats, or trap bar pulls. This pattern allows both lifts to be trained frequently enough for progression, but without constant maximal effort.

Another key modification involves rep schemes. Traditional PPL programming defaults to 8–12 reps per set, which is ideal for hypertrophy but suboptimal for building maximal strength. In a strength-adapted PPL, primary lifts shift to 3–6 reps per set at intensities between 75% and 90% of one-rep max. Secondary lifts might occupy the 6–10 rep range, and accessories remain higher to support joint health and musculature. This graduated intensity curve—heavy compounds, moderate secondary lifts, light accessories—creates a pyramid of fatigue management within each session, enabling the lifter to drive adaptation without compromising longevity.

Exercise selection, too, must reflect the goal. A hypertrophy PPL split might include cable flyes, machine rows, or hip thrusts—not inherently bad choices, but inefficient for strength training. Instead, lifters should prioritize barbell and free-weight movements that require stabilization, coordination, and load progression. Presses, squats, rows, and pulls from various angles should dominate the program. Isolation movements can still appear, but as joint protectors and weak-point builders, not as primary training stimuli. The difference lies in purpose. Strength training does not exclude assistance work—it merely subordinates it.

Progression models must also shift. In hypertrophy PPLs, progress is often measured in added sets, reps, or exercises. In strength-focused training, the metric is bar speed, mechanical efficiency, and load. Linear progression, double progression, and wave loading schemes can all work within a PPL framework, provided they're applied to the main lifts and not buried under layers of fatigue-inducing volume. The lifter's weekly question is no longer "Did I train every muscle twice?" but "Did my top sets move better, cleaner, or heavier than last week?" If the answer is no, the split needs retooling—not more accessory fluff.

One structural limitation of PPL for strength is its lack of a built-in system for movement pattern overlap. Unlike Upper/Lower splits, which often pair squat and hinge or push and pull variations in the same week for balance, PPL segments those patterns into isolated silos. This works against the specificity demands of competitive strength sports. A powerlifter, for example, must train the squat, bench, and deadlift multiple times per week with variations to reinforce technique under different loads and conditions. A strict PPL makes this difficult unless supplemented with hybrid days or modified session design. For general strength, however— particularly for non-competitive lifters—PPL can still function if the variations are programmed wisely.

Fatigue monitoring becomes critical. Strength training pushes the nervous system, not just the muscles. Poor sleep, stress, and joint pain are not background noise—they're signals that intensity must be dialed back. In high-frequency PPL setups, these signals often arrive too late, masked by hypertrophy-style session design that rewards effort over output. Strength progress depends on the opposite: clear metrics, unambiguous feedback, and the discipline to back off when movement quality degrades. A lifter running PPL for strength must accept that some weeks, fewer reps or sets are a victory if the top lifts are improving.

The psychology of the split also matters. Strength requires patience. Many lifters attracted to PPL come from a hypertrophy background, where each session feels productive—high reps, pump-driven finishers, visible muscular fatigue. Strength training lacks this immediacy. Some days involve five heavy sets and little else. There is no dramatic fatigue, no skin-splitting pump. Progress is hidden in bar speed, technical sharpness, or improved setup. A lifter who fails to adjust expectations will misinterpret effective strength sessions as "not enough," and add unnecessary work that erodes the goal.

PPL can be repurposed for strength—but not without changes. It must be slowed, stripped down, and restructured around load, not fatigue. Volume must be managed, rest intervals respected, and exercise selection tightened. The split's segmented design becomes a tool for focused intensity, not a container for maximal training density. Used correctly, it can build general strength effectively for lifters who value structure and movement specificity. Used carelessly, it becomes a hypertrophy template wearing a strength badge.

In the end, PPL for strength gains is less about what's on the paper and more about how it's executed. The split provides a scaffold. The lifter provides the discipline. Only one of those can make the bar move heavier over time.

Chapter 13: When PPL Becomes a Trap

For all its structural logic and hypertrophy potential, the Push/Pull/Legs split carries a darker edge rarely discussed in the influencer-curated highlight reels: its tendency to become a self-imposed trap. What begins as a sensible training framework often morphs into an unsustainable cycle of overcommitment, fatigue, and stagnation—not because the split is broken, but because it invites the lifter to bury themselves in volume without questioning whether they can actually recover from it. When lifters confuse ambition with output, frequency with discipline, and volume with necessity, PPL turns from a tool into a treadmill—perpetual motion with no forward progress.

The trap begins with expectation. The standard PPL rotation—six days per week, each muscle group trained twice—is seductive. It sounds efficient, intelligent, and serious. Training nearly every day creates the illusion of progress through effort. And in the first few weeks, that illusion holds. Muscles feel full, soreness is manageable, and motivation is high. But adaptation is not linear. The body does not scale recovery at the same rate volume increases. The nervous system and connective tissue adapt more slowly than muscle. By the time the external signs of fatigue arrive—stagnant lifts, nagging joint pain, trouble sleeping—the damage is already accumulating under the surface.

The first crack is usually inconsistency. Life interrupts the idealized six-day cycle. A missed session becomes a scheduling puzzle. Should the lifter double up the next day? Skip it and continue the rotation? Start the week over? This indecision reveals the first flaw: PPL is unforgiving when not run in perfect sequence. Its segmented structure—Push, Pull, Legs—requires that each day follow the last without disruption for weekly balance to hold. When reality intervenes, the structure fractures. Most lifters lack the experience to adapt it on the fly, so they either restart unnecessarily or press forward with poor sequencing that overtaxes already fatigued systems.

But even when the schedule holds, the trap deepens through mismanaged fatigue. High-frequency training requires careful attention to recovery variables—sleep, nutrition, stress management, and intra-week intensity modulation. Most lifters, motivated by the aesthetic demands of hypertrophy, simply don't adjust. Every Push day includes flat bench, incline work, overhead pressing, triceps, and laterals. Every Pull day becomes a smorgasbord of rows, pull-ups, face pulls, curls, and shrugs. Leg days attempt to cram in all squats, hinges, lunges, and isolation work under one roof. The result isn't growth—it's diminishing returns masked as effort.

Without rest days strategically inserted, cumulative fatigue begins to mask performance. Lifters still show up, still complete the workout, but load progression stalls. Reps flatten. RPE climbs even as the weight remains static. The sessions still feel hard, so they're interpreted as productive, but the training effect is gone. Without realizing it, the lifter has traded progression for maintenance while expending maximum effort. This condition, often described as "functional overreaching," is a precursor to full burnout if not corrected. And PPL, with its tight six-day loop and expectation of constant output, often accelerates that slide.

Mentally, the trap is just as insidious. PPL encourages a sense of routine devotion. Each day has its identity: Push, Pull, Legs. Miss one and the rhythm feels broken. Lifters begin to equate adherence with discipline, failing to recognize when the structure itself is the problem. The fear of losing progress drives them to complete sessions regardless of sleep quality, joint pain, or systemic fatigue. Eventually, workouts shift from being stimulus-focused to box-checking routines. The intensity is there, but not the intent. Effort becomes divorced from outcome.

In this state, training becomes reactive. Instead of adjusting based on readiness or objective feedback, the lifter grinds forward, mistaking the exhaustion as a sign of virtue. Worse still, the fix often pursued is more volume. If growth has stalled, surely the problem is that the back isn't getting enough work, or that arms need a separate day. This logic leads to hybridized monstrosities—PPL with added arm days, or seven-day "bro PPL" rotations. These are not solutions; they are escape tunnels that lead deeper into the trap, delaying the confrontation with what's actually failing: recovery.

Another subtle consequence of the PPL trap is neglect of movement balance. The format, by design, splits training into pressing, pulling, and lower-body sessions. Over time, lifters often begin to favor one session type over the others—more pressing variations, fewer vertical pulls, neglect of posterior chain work. This skew creeps in gradually. Pressing numbers improve, but rows stagnate. Deadlift variations disappear because they compromise squatting performance. Curls and triceps work multiply, while direct hamstring and calf work vanish. The split's structure makes it easy to rationalize these imbalances—each day has its theme—but the long-term outcome is clear: muscular asymmetry, movement dysfunction, and joint irritation.

Even those who manage to maintain balance eventually hit the wall of diminishing returns. The six-day frequency that initially delivered rapid gains starts to blunt sensitivity to training stimuli. For natural lifters, this is inevitable. The body adapts not just to the weight, but to the routine itself. Repeating the same movement patterns with the same frequency and effort week after week reduces novelty, diminishes tension stimulus, and desensitizes hypertrophic pathways. The split that once felt optimal now feels obligatory. Progress slows, but the routine is too ingrained to abandon. This is the final layer of the trap: attachment.

Lifters become loyal to the identity of training six days a week. To scale back feels like regression, not adjustment. To deload feels like weakness. The idea of moving to a four-day Upper/Lower split or a three-day full-body program is viewed not as a strategic decision, but as a personal failing. PPL becomes a belief system—one that must be defended even when it no longer delivers results. The lifter keeps going, convinced that fatigue is a rite of passage, that soreness is proof, that volume is the answer. By the time injuries or burnout force change, the damage—physiological or psychological—is already done.

Avoiding the trap doesn't mean abandoning PPL. It means understanding its limits. A six-day rotation should be earned, not assumed. It should follow a buildup of training experience, load tolerance, and recovery management—not replace them. Strategic rest days must be built in, either through a 3-on/1-off pattern or by reducing frequency to five or even four days. Volume should be scaled not to match online templates, but to reflect actual performance—bar speed, rep quality, and recovery metrics. The split should be periodized, not repeated indefinitely. Rotations of rep schemes, movement emphasis, and even full-split cycles are necessary to keep adaptation moving forward.

PPL is not a trap by design—it becomes one when lifters treat it as a destination rather than a tool. It succeeds when applied intelligently, adjusted to life circumstances, and allowed to evolve. But when it's treated as gospel—non-negotiable, unmodifiable, and perpetually ideal—it becomes the very thing it was meant to prevent: a rigid, unsustainable grind disguised as optimal training. The moment a split stops serving the lifter and starts dictating their training life, it ceases to be a method and becomes a mistake. And like all traps, the only way out begins with realizing you're already in it.

Chapter 14: The Case for Full-Body Simplicity

In a fitness culture increasingly obsessed with fragmentation—dividing muscles into days, days into blocks, and blocks into microcycles—the appeal of full-body training almost feels subversive. It resists specialization. It ignores aesthetic compartmentalization. It flies in the face of "serious lifter" orthodoxy that equates complexity with advancement. But the case for full-body training is not a nostalgic return to beginner routines or a concession to minimalism. It's a strategic recalibration, rooted in efficiency, recoverability, and progression. And for lifters willing to challenge the dogma of isolation, it offers a clear alternative to the fatigue-laden grind of more elaborate splits.

Full-body simplicity is not simplicity by omission—it's simplicity by design. A full-body session doesn't mean three random lifts slapped together. It means selecting key movements that target multiple muscle groups across planes of motion, structuring sessions that maximize systemic output without overwhelming any single region. Done well, full-body training stimulates every major muscle group with high efficiency, supports recovery through intelligent volume control, and allows for consistent progression with fewer sessions. This is not a fallback option for people who can't "commit" to six days a week. It's a structure that commits fully to stimulus quality over schedule intensity.

The primary advantage of full-body training is frequency. Every muscle group is stimulated multiple times per week, often three, without requiring marathon sessions or redundant volume. For natural lifters, this frequency is not just adequate—it's ideal. Hypertrophy and strength both benefit from regular exposure to compound lifts under varied loads and tempos. Full-body sessions naturally accommodate this by necessity. The squat, bench, deadlift, row, pull-up, and overhead press can all find a place across three weekly sessions, each with different emphasis or loading scheme. Rather than isolating a muscle group once per week and hoping for maximal fiber recruitment, full-body training distributes volume across repeated efforts, each more recoverable than a singular onslaught.

This repetition also improves technical proficiency. Strength is a skill, and skills are honed through frequency. A lifter who squats three times per week—even with varying intensity and volume—develops patterning, efficiency, and bar control at a faster rate than someone squatting once weekly. The same is true for pressing, pulling, and hinging. Full-body training doesn't just build the body—it trains the brain. The nervous system becomes more efficient, movement quality improves, and injury risk declines. Especially for intermediate lifters who've outgrown linear progression but aren't ready for heavy periodization, this exposure creates a platform for consistent, sustainable improvement.

From a fatigue management perspective, full-body training excels precisely because it limits excess. When programming only three or four working sets per muscle group per session, volume remains high enough for adaptation but low enough to avoid burnout. There's little temptation to stack six pressing variations or annihilate the posterior chain in one go. Each muscle gets a piece of the pie, not the entire pie. This restraint leads to surprisingly durable training—less soreness, more consistent output, fewer missed sessions due to residual fatigue or joint discomfort. It also promotes better recovery without needing excessive rest days, making it ideal for lifters with jobs, families, and actual responsibilities.

Time efficiency is another critical advantage. A well-structured full-body session—60 to 75 minutes, three times a week—delivers nearly all of the benefits of higher-frequency splits without monopolizing the week. This matters for lifters whose lives cannot accommodate six-day training schedules. Rather than struggling to make PPL "fit" into an erratic calendar, full-body training provides a flexible, high-yield framework that delivers results without demanding a lifestyle overhaul. Miss one session and very little is lost—every workout trains the entire body, so nothing is stranded for seven days. That continuity, absent in more fragmented splits, protects consistency even when the calendar doesn't cooperate.

Critically, full-body simplicity does not mean full-body monotony. Sessions can and should vary across the week. Monday might emphasize heavy squatting and horizontal pressing. Wednesday might prioritize deadlift variations and vertical pulls. Friday can rotate toward overhead pressing and single-leg work. Accessories can shift in each session to address different planes of motion or weak points—rear delts one day, triceps the next, calves another. Across the week, each movement pattern is trained multiple times, but not identically. This creates a wave-like stimulus—varied enough to prevent staleness, consistent enough to drive adaptation.

Even from a hypertrophy perspective—where PPL is often treated as gospel—full-body training holds more potential than it's given credit for. While it doesn't allow for the same session density per muscle group, it compensates with distributed quality. Muscles are trained when fresh, not buried under five preceding exercises. Effort and load remain high. Over the course of the week, the total weekly volume can match or exceed that of more traditional splits, particularly when accessories are rotated intelligently. For natural lifters, who thrive on frequency and recoverability more than sheer isolation, this model supports both size and performance without overreaching.

There's also a psychological liberation to full-body training. Without the weight of overly segmented expectations—"today is arm day, tomorrow is back day"—each session becomes a focused, efficient opportunity to improve. This minimizes performance anxiety, reduces session-to-session pressure, and improves long-term adherence. When training is simplified, execution improves. Fewer decisions, fewer distractions, fewer excuses. The lifter shows up, trains the entire body, and leaves knowing that no region has been neglected and no session wasted. That sense of systemic training, of integrated effort, keeps momentum alive even when life threatens to intervene.

This structure also encourages smarter periodization. Because each movement pattern appears multiple times per week, intensities and rep schemes can be cycled within the same week. One day might focus on heavy triples for the squat, another on moderate-volume sets of eight. This intra-week variation delivers the benefits of undulating periodization—novelty, recovery modulation, and broad adaptation—without requiring wholesale structural changes or mesocycle overhauls. It's simple in structure but complex in application, allowing for nuance without dependence on a calendar-based progression model.

Of course, full-body training is not without limitations. It demands discipline in exercise selection and restraint in volume. There is no room for fluff. Every movement must earn its place. There's less opportunity for body-part pampering or novelty-based programming. Lifters obsessed with direct work for every visible muscle may feel constrained. But these are not flaws of the split—they're features. They filter out the noise and force lifters to prioritize what actually drives adaptation:

compound lifts, progressive loading, and consistent effort across time.

The case for full-body simplicity is not a rejection of advanced training. It's a rejection of needless complexity. In a landscape where every training plan seems to require six days, ten exercises, and fifty weekly sets per muscle group, full-body training offers a refreshing reminder that effectiveness isn't measured by volume—it's measured by results. For lifters with limited time, finite recovery, or simply a desire to train hard without drowning in minutiae, full-body simplicity delivers not just adequacy, but excellence.

It doesn't demand perfect conditions. It doesn't require exhaustive variation. It asks only for consistency, focus, and the humility to do less—but better. And in that, it may be the most advanced split of all.

Chapter 15: Full-Body for the Busy and the Brave

For lifters pressed for time, full-body training offers more than just convenience—it offers proof that efficiency, not frequency, is the true gatekeeper of progress. The modern obsession with high-frequency, body-part-specific splits feeds the illusion that more sessions equal better results, when in reality, it's the quality and sustainability of training that determine long-term adaptation. Full-body training respects the finite nature of time, energy, and recovery. It doesn't ask the lifter to structure life around training—it structures training around life. And that subtle inversion makes it the most pragmatic—and perhaps the most brutally honest—approach available to lifters who want to grow stronger, bigger, or more resilient without surrendering their schedule.

For the time-constrained, full-body training is not a compromise—it's a distillation. The lifter shows up three or four days a week, hits the entire body each session, and leaves knowing that no major muscle group or pattern has been neglected. This consolidation minimizes the decision fatigue inherent in more complex splits. There's no mental overhead spent wondering whether to squeeze in calves on back day or whether triceps were sufficiently trained two days ago. Everything gets trained. Every time. This simplicity doesn't just save time; it saves willpower, which, for most busy lifters, is in shorter supply than motivation.

But full-body training isn't just for the overscheduled—it's for the brave. Because it strips away the rituals that many lifters lean on to feel "in control." Gone are the long, leisurely workouts built around five angles of chest or 20-set back days followed by redundant biceps fluff. Full-body training asks the uncomfortable question: What actually matters? And the answer is never ten isolation movements or three hours of chasing fatigue. The answer is compound lifts, executed with effort, intensity, and consistency. It's not less demanding. It's less indulgent.

Three full-body sessions per week, intelligently programmed, can match or exceed the training stimulus of six-day splits. But it requires an uncomfortable level of focus. There's no room for wasted sets or casual warm-up reps masquerading as work. Each session must deliver a potent blend of mechanical tension, movement diversity, and volume density. A Monday might open with squats, follow with a vertical press and horizontal pull, then close with targeted accessory work for posterior chain or delts. Wednesday might pivot to deadlifts, bench press, and pull-ups. Friday shifts to front squats, overhead pressing, and barbell rows. Across the week, every major movement pattern is hit with meaningful load and variation.

This rotation creates a rhythmic training cadence where each session builds upon the last without duplication. Muscles are stimulated frequently but not fatigued excessively. Sessions remain under 75 minutes, but contain everything necessary for progression. The trick is not in doing more work—it's in selecting the right work and executing it without compromise. This forces the lifter to train with intent. Every lift counts. There is no back-end fluff to hide behind if effort is lacking on the main movements. In this way, full-body training develops not just the physique but the discipline of lifters who are no longer able—or willing—to live in the gym.

Recovery, paradoxically, improves under full-body programming for those with demanding lives. Training three or four non-consecutive days per week allows for regular systemic deloading without needing formal taper weeks. Joints aren't hammered by consecutive high-load days. Sleep debt, work stress, and inconsistent nutrition—all realities for non-professionals—are absorbed more easily by a structure that doesn't presume daily readiness. Unlike six-day splits, where a single bad night can sabotage multiple sessions, full-body plans build in space for recalibration. Progress isn't built on heroic single sessions but on sustainable repetition. For those working 50-hour weeks, raising kids, or managing variable schedules, this flexibility isn't just helpful—it's necessary.

Even in advanced training contexts, full-body simplicity remains potent. Olympic weightlifters, long before the rise of YouTube programs and hypertrophy spreadsheets, trained with full-body principles because their sport demanded it. Squats, pulls, and presses appeared in every session, varied by intensity and speed, not by isolated focus. The logic wasn't aesthetic—it was developmental. Skill acquisition, strength maintenance, and movement proficiency all benefit from frequency. That same logic applies to lifters chasing physique or general performance goals. Training the body as a system, repeatedly, develops systemic capacity—coordination, work tolerance, and resilience—that fragmented splits often neglect.

There's also a psychological recalibration that occurs under full-body training. The lifter no longer thinks in muscle groups but in movement patterns. They stop asking, "What am I training today?" and start asking, "How will I move today?" This perspective shift has consequences. Training becomes more performance-oriented, less cosmetic. Progress is measured in load, tempo, range, and fatigue resistance—not pump or burn. This mindset not only improves training quality but reduces anxiety around missed sessions. If you train full-body three times a week and miss one, the entire body has still been trained twice. No backlog, no panic. Just continuity.

That continuity is perhaps full-body training's most underrated feature. While six-day splits buckle under disruption, full-body structures adapt seamlessly. If one session is missed, it's folded into the next. If only two sessions can be completed that week, no muscle group is left behind. The program bends, but never breaks. This durability is what keeps progress on track when life becomes unpredictable. It respects the reality that most lifters are not in control of their calendar. It doesn't penalize inconsistency—it designs for it.

There are, of course, trade-offs. Full-body training offers less room for specialization. A lifter who wants to bring up a single body part to disproportionate size might struggle within a constrained session. There is limited time for exhaustive arm work or multiple chest angles. But these limitations are often self-imposed expectations masquerading as requirements. Most lifters don't need specialization—they need consistency. They don't need 20 sets for arms—they need five done properly, repeated weekly. Full-body simplicity doesn't prevent growth; it removes the illusion that growth requires theatrical effort rather than disciplined output.

Ultimately, full-body training for the busy and the brave isn't about doing the minimum. It's about doing the maximum with the minimum distraction. It asks for less time but demands more intention. It refuses to equate effort with exhaustion, volume with virtue, or complexity with advancement. It forces the lifter to examine what actually drives results: movement quality, load progression, and adherence over time. And it builds a training habit that is as resilient as it is effective.

In a world that markets complexity as progress, full-body training remains the quiet rebuttal. It is not for those who need to feel busy to feel productive. It is for those willing to strip training down to its essentials and ask: what actually moves the needle? For the lifter who lives a full life outside the gym but still wants meaningful results within it, full-body training is not a compromise. It's the answer.

Chapter 16: Programming a Full-Body Plan

Programming a full-body training plan begins with rejecting the assumption that simplicity equals randomness. The appeal of training the entire body in one session often misleads lifters into thinking that any three to five compound lifts strung together will produce results. In reality, effective full-body programming requires more planning than most splits because it demands balance across planes of motion, movement patterns, and fatigue variables—all within a single, limited session. Without that planning, full-body sessions turn into chaotic assemblies of effort with no progression logic. The goal isn't to hit everything every time; it's to construct a rhythm of sessions that systematically stress each pattern and muscle group across the week with enough variety to stimulate adaptation without drifting into inconsistency.

A well-structured full-body week usually comprises three or four training sessions. Each session needs a distinct primary focus—heavy lift, volume lift, or technical lift—to avoid redundancy and allow meaningful intensity without chronic overload. For instance, Monday might be the heavy day: squats, barbell bench press, and weighted chin-ups, each performed for low-to-moderate reps at high load. Wednesday becomes a volume day: Romanian deadlifts, dumbbell incline press, and high-rep rows, all with more controlled tempo and shorter rest. Friday might rotate in unilateral work—front-foot elevated split squats, single-arm landmine press, and inverted rows—alongside targeted isolation for hamstrings, delts, and calves.

This microcycle accomplishes a complete training stimulus without hammering the same muscles or joints repetitively.

Movement pattern allocation is foundational. Every week should cover knee-dominant and hip-dominant lower-body patterns, horizontal and vertical pushing and pulling, core stabilization, and unilateral work. But not all of that needs to be crammed into every session. One session might focus on knee-dominant squatting and horizontal pressing, another on hip-dominant hinging and vertical pulling. This distribution maintains balance while keeping sessions under 75 minutes. Attempting to train every pattern equally in every workout not only leads to fatigue overflow but diminishes the attention any one movement can receive. Full-body training is systemic in scope, but selective in execution.

Exercise selection should be ruthlessly utilitarian. In a full-body program, there's no room for redundancy. The lifts must carry both mechanical efficiency and broad training effect. For most lifters, that means building each session around one or two major compound lifts—squat, deadlift, bench, overhead press, chin-up, row—and filling remaining time with accessories that either address weak points or provide movement contrast. For example, pairing a heavy barbell squat with dumbbell incline press and a cable row allows for maximal lower-body stimulus, effective upper-body pressing, and posterior chain engagement—all without overwhelming the spine or shoulder joints with repetitive stress.

Progression models must adapt to the full-body format. Because most major lifts are trained at least twice weekly, classic linear progression quickly exhausts its utility. Instead, rotating intensity across sessions provides more sustainable stimulus.

Monday's squat might be heavy for triples; Friday's might be tempo-based for sets of eight. Both drive adaptation, but through different pathways—mechanical load and metabolic fatigue. This variation doesn't just prevent plateau; it also distributes recovery demand more intelligently, allowing lifters to train hard without inviting joint stress or CNS fatigue.

Volume in full-body training is managed weekly, not daily. A single session might include only two sets of pulling, three of pressing, and three of lower-body work, which feels light in isolation but adds up over multiple sessions. A trap many lifters fall into is attempting to match per-session volume from their previous split. This leads to bloated workouts and overuse injuries. The correct approach is to think in terms of "exposure per pattern per week." If horizontal pressing appears in two sessions, each with three quality sets, that's six meaningful exposures—enough to drive progress without needing a chest-only day.

One of the most overlooked aspects of full-body programming is movement redundancy across the week. It's easy to repeat similar mechanics under different names. A back squat on Monday and a front squat on Friday may appear different but both stress the quads and spinal extensors. Similarly, bench press and overhead press share triceps and anterior deltoid loading. If both lifts are pushed hard in close succession without managing volume or load, cumulative fatigue outpaces recovery. This is where strategic variation matters. Instead of heavy overhead pressing after a demanding bench session, choose a landmine press or incline dumbbell variation with less joint stress and a different loading curve.

Accessory work in full-body training serves two purposes: stimulus support and recovery preservation. It targets areas undertrained by big lifts—rear delts, hamstrings, core, calves—without adding unnecessary fatigue. These movements should be rotated weekly and matched to the session's theme. On a volume day, accessories might lean higher in reps with controlled tempo. On a heavy day, they might skew lower in reps with greater focus on load and bar speed. These subtle adjustments keep fatigue in check while preserving hypertrophic stimulus across minor muscle groups often missed in minimalist templates.

Rest periods must also reflect session intent. A Monday session built around low-rep barbell lifts requires full rest between sets—2 to 4 minutes—to maintain output. A Wednesday session built around higher rep ranges and accessory supersets might use shorter rest intervals to condense workload and raise metabolic stress. These aren't just practical adjustments—they're strategic tools for regulating fatigue and training effect. Full-body training doesn't lend itself well to auto-piloted rest. The pacing of a session is as critical as its structure.

Conditioning and energy system work can coexist with full-body training but must be dosed carefully. A common mistake is stacking HIIT or conditioning circuits onto already dense full-body sessions. The result isn't conditioning—it's interference. Instead, conditioning should be programmed on off days or as brief, separate sessions, especially for lifters chasing both strength and hypertrophy. When used intra-session, it should be structured to avoid conflicting with primary movement goals—sled pushes after squats, for instance, rather than before.

Deloading is another structural necessity. In higher-frequency training, fatigue often signals when a deload is overdue. In full-body plans, cumulative fatigue sneaks in quieter. Because no single area is crushed in isolation, overall stress accumulates more slowly, but still steadily. Every fourth to sixth week should see a planned reduction in either volume or intensity. This could mean reducing top set loads by 10–15%, trimming accessories, or dropping a session altogether. This keeps progress linear and joint integrity intact—especially for lifters training around age, injury history, or limited recovery bandwidth.

Perhaps most importantly, full-body programming demands personal honesty. It forces lifters to acknowledge which movements they've been avoiding, which patterns dominate their split, and where weaknesses hide. It removes the comfort of isolation and replaces it with systemic responsibility. A full-body plan will not tolerate poor recovery, inconsistent effort, or sloppy execution. But when approached with intention, it delivers more training effect per session than any split can match—and it does so without pretending that most lifters have unlimited time, perfect recovery, or a professional athlete's schedule.

Programming a full-body plan is not about doing everything—it's about doing enough of the right things, repeatedly, with precision. It's a system that respects both physiology and practicality. When done right, it becomes the most honest expression of training: not fragmented, not glorified busyness, but focused, adaptable work that yields results across time. The complexity of the human body doesn't require complexity in planning—it requires structure, progression, and above all, restraint. And that's where full-body training excels.

Chapter 17: Full-Body for Mass and Balance

The hypertrophy potential of full-body training is often misunderstood—not because it lacks efficacy, but because it refuses to conform to bodybuilding's most popular narrative: the idea that more is more, and that muscle groups need their own day to "grow properly." In contrast, full-body training distributes hypertrophic stimulus evenly across the week, prioritizing total volume, movement diversity, and fatigue management over the illusion of specialization. For the lifter seeking muscular growth that is balanced, sustainable, and resistant to burnout, full-body training offers a streamlined, system-wide approach that builds not just size, but a resilient and proportionate physique.

The mechanics of full-body hypertrophy begin with frequency. By targeting each major muscle group two to three times per week, full-body programs capitalize on what the literature consistently shows: muscles respond more favorably to frequent, moderately dosed stimulation than to infrequent, high-volume bombardment. Each exposure doesn't need to be maximal; it just needs to be consistent and recoverable. This approach increases total weekly effective reps, improves movement skill under tension, and raises the quality of output across the mesocycle. Instead of incinerating a muscle group once every seven days with 20 sets, full-body training applies six to eight high-quality sets multiple times a week—delivering the same or greater growth stimulus with less peripheral fatigue.

This distribution also mitigates a common flaw in body-part splits: the trade-off between fatigue and movement quality. In a traditional chest day, the bench press is often followed by incline presses, flyes, dips, and push-ups. By the second or third exercise, fatigue is no longer local—it's systemic. Stabilizers are compromised, joint wear accumulates, and effort is misallocated. In full-body training, however, muscles are hit earlier in the session, when they're fresh. A bench press on Monday and an overhead press on Thursday both benefit from reduced cumulative fatigue, leading to better mechanics, more consistent force output, and, ultimately, better muscle fiber recruitment across sets.

Balanced development is another strength of full-body hypertrophy programming. Traditional splits often overemphasize mirror muscles—chest, biceps, shoulders—while neglecting less glamorous but structurally essential regions like hamstrings, mid-back, and deep core. Because full-body training requires deliberate allocation of movement patterns, it naturally reinforces symmetry. A session cannot be built around six pressing variations because there isn't time. Every lift must earn its place, and if hamstrings or rear delts have been ignored, the deficiency becomes obvious within a few sessions. This enforced economy creates more proportional development—not from aesthetics alone, but from structural necessity.

That structural balance extends to movement patterning. A full-body plan, by design, must integrate horizontal and vertical pushing and pulling, squatting and hinging, unilateral and bilateral work. A program that includes trap-bar deadlifts, incline dumbbell presses, chin-ups, Bulgarian split squats, and landmine rows over the course of the week provides a more comprehensive muscular stimulus than a split focused on isolating each part for volume's sake. This systemic approach builds coordination and connective integrity alongside hypertrophy. The result is not just muscle mass, but muscle mass applied across functional, load-bearing patterns—a crucial distinction for long-term progress and joint health.

Volume remains the driving force behind hypertrophy, but in full-body programming, that volume must be curated, not accumulated indiscriminately. Most lifters can tolerate between 10 and 20 sets per muscle group per week, depending on training age, recovery bandwidth, and proximity to failure. Full-body splits allow these sets to be spread across three to four exposures, reducing per-session joint strain and improving set quality. A lifter might perform three sets of squats on Monday, RDLs on Wednesday, and leg presses on Friday. Each session is manageable; none feel excessive. Yet the weekly lower-body volume matches, and often surpasses, what would be crammed into a singular "leg day."

Load and rep scheme variation also enhances hypertrophy outcomes within a full-body plan. One exposure per week might use moderate loads (8–12 reps) to emphasize mechanical tension and metabolic fatigue. Another might employ slightly higher reps (12–15) with controlled tempo for sarcoplasmic expansion and joint-friendly volume. A third exposure might rotate in lower-rep, higher-load work (5–8) to maintain neural drive and reinforce strength in compound movements. This undulating structure creates stimulus diversity without violating the consistency required for muscle growth. Muscles are challenged across fiber types, energy systems, and rep ranges—all while preserving movement proficiency.

This rotational structure also allows for strategic emphasis without wholesale specialization. If a lifter wants to bring up their back or posterior chain, additional volume can be slotted into the accessory portion of each session. More pull variations, rear delt raises, or hip extensions can be distributed subtly throughout the week without compromising overall balance. Unlike body-part splits, where specialization requires adding entire training days or cannibalizing others, full-body plans allow for surgical adjustments. This targeted insertion of volume, when programmed intelligently, enhances weak points without derailing systemic recovery.

Progression in full-body hypertrophy training hinges on execution and consistency, not novelty. Each movement should appear frequently enough to allow technical refinement and load progression, but not so often that recovery falters. Tracking a select set of compound lifts—bench, squat, chin-up, row, overhead press—and rotating accessory work every few weeks enables long-term overload without stagnation. The goal isn't to constantly change exercises but to extract more from each one: smoother reps, better range, cleaner lockouts, slower eccentrics. This rep-level precision, often lost in volume-chasing programs, is central to muscle fiber recruitment and adaptation.

Recovery between sessions is another hidden advantage. Full-body plans, spread over three or four days with rest between, respect the nervous system's limits. They allow for adaptation rather than accumulation of stress. Lifters who follow traditional splits often report chronic tightness, joint discomfort, or low-grade burnout—not because the volume is too high in absolute terms, but because it's compressed into narrow windows and repeated weekly without modulation. Full-body training, by contrast, gives the body room to absorb work and grow. It emphasizes signal clarity over signal intensity.

There's also an underestimated mental benefit. Full-body training reduces the emotional load of missed sessions. In a split routine, missing "back day" can feel catastrophic, requiring reordering of the entire week. In a full-body plan, each session trains every major region. Miss a day and you're still 66 percent compliant. The plan stays intact. This reduces the stress of perfectionism and supports long-term adherence—a critical factor in hypertrophy, where months, not weeks, determine meaningful outcomes.

Finally, full-body training removes the illusion of "muscle ownership." In split routines, lifters often treat each muscle group as a separate project, divorced from the rest of the system. Chest day is about chest. Leg day is about legs. But in reality, hypertrophy occurs within a systemic context: joints must remain stable, movement patterns efficient, recovery balanced. Full-body training enforces this reality. It doesn't allow the lifter to isolate themselves into imbalance. It asks not how much you can do for your biceps, but how much your entire system can recover from while still progressing.

Full-body training for mass and balance is not a niche option for time-starved generalists. It is a methodical, high-signal strategy for building muscular size across the entire body with minimal redundancy and maximal recoverability. It avoids the traps of overcomplication, fragmentation, and recovery neglect. And it builds lifters who are not only bigger—but better built. Proportional. Functional. Durable. Because the point of hypertrophy is not to isolate muscle from the body—but to build a body that is strong, capable, and whole.

Chapter 18: Full-Body for Strength

Full-body training is where strength development meets structural integrity. While hypertrophy protocols are often cluttered with mechanical variation and aesthetic prioritization, strength training has no such luxury—it demands precision, frequency, and repetition. And full-body programming, when constructed intelligently, offers the most direct path to these outcomes. It provides the structure to train key lifts multiple times per week, the space to emphasize neural output over fatigue, and the rhythm necessary to build technical fluency under load. For lifters focused on raw strength—whether in the squat, deadlift, press, or pull—full-body training is not just viable. It is, in many respects, optimal.

The strength-building case for full-body training begins with its frequency. To lift heavier, one must lift often. Neural adaptations—the true engine of strength—respond to repeated exposure, not sporadic intensity. A lifter who squats once per week has fewer opportunities to refine mechanics, build motor patterning, and reinforce bracing than one who squats two or three times. Full-body programming naturally integrates this exposure. A Monday session might include high-bar squats, Wednesday a paused front squat, Friday a box squat. Each variant reinforces the core movement while targeting slightly different mechanics or weak points. The result is technical refinement alongside progressive overload—a dual stimulus rarely sustained in less frequent splits.

This exposure also allows for strategic load modulation across the week, which is essential for sustainable strength gains. Rather than attempting maximal output in a single, overloaded session, full-body plans distribute intensity. A heavy triple on Monday, a submaximal five-rep wave midweek, and a speed-based variation on Friday spread both neural and mechanical stress while maintaining high-quality execution. This prevents the stagnation and breakdown often seen in once-a-week powerlifting templates, where every effort is maximal, and every repetition must bear the full burden of weekly progress.

Beyond frequency, full-body strength training enforces movement balance. Strength is not built in isolation. A deadlift doesn't improve because you train your back—it improves because your grip, core, glutes, hamstrings, and thoracic extensors all rise together. A press isn't limited by triceps size, but by scapular control, lat engagement, and core stability. Full-body sessions demand attention to these systems. No movement can be skipped without exposing its absence in a following lift. That interdependence sharpens programming instincts. It forces the lifter to consider how today's hinge affects tomorrow's squat, how fatigue from rows may interfere with pressing form, and where a weak link might compromise force transfer.

Structurally, a full-body strength session begins with a priority lift—usually a compound barbell movement trained for low reps (3–6) at moderate to high intensity (75–90% 1RM). This is the training engine. Squats, deadlifts, bench presses, overhead presses, barbell rows, and weighted chins all fit here, rotated intelligently across the week. Following that lift is a secondary movement—often a variation or complementary pattern—trained for moderate reps (6–8) and slightly lower intensity. This preserves the movement's relevance while reducing systemic cost. Finally, the session ends with two to three accessories targeting weak links: rear delts, glutes, core, or grip. These are not tacked-on fluff but high-signal additions that preserve joint integrity and prevent regression.

Rest intervals in these sessions are long and deliberate. Two to four minutes for primary lifts, sometimes more, with reduced rest only introduced for accessory work. Unlike hypertrophy training, where metabolic fatigue can serve as a secondary stimulus, strength training depends on force output—and that means full recovery between sets. Rushing the rest sabotages not just performance but the very adaptation being chased: maximal force expression under heavy load.

Volume, in this context, is weaponized sparingly. More is not better. Better is better. Most strength-focused full-body sessions include three to five exercises total, with six to ten hard sets aimed at reinforcing movement quality and bar speed. Any more and intensity suffers. Any less and skill acquisition stalls. This tension between doing enough and doing too much is the defining characteristic of elite-level programming. Full-body strength plans walk this line precisely because they encourage economy. There is no space for fluff. Every set must matter. Every rep must be accounted for.

Importantly, full-body training enables specificity without rigidity. Because the same movement patterns recur throughout the week, variations can be introduced without disrupting continuity. A Monday deadlift might be from the floor, heavy and conventional. Wednesday introduces Romanian deadlifts at higher reps for hamstring development. Friday rotates in trap-bar pulls for speed and lockout mechanics. The deadlift is trained three times, but never identically. This increases neural efficiency, enhances weak point targeting, and reduces the monotony that often creeps into specialized strength templates.

Periodization in a full-body context also gains depth. Weekly undulating models—where intensity, volume, and focus rotate session to session—become easier to implement. A squat might follow a 3x3 model on Monday, an 8-rep tempo variant on Wednesday, and a paused 5x5 on Friday. Each session builds on the last, not in a linear progression, but in a wave that drives long-term gains while preserving freshness. These microcycles can be further layered into mesocycles that alternate between accumulation and intensification blocks, seamlessly integrated into the full-body rhythm.

Recovery is where full-body training surprises most lifters. Despite training major lifts every session, systemic fatigue is often lower than in specialized splits. Why? Because the load is distributed. No single session annihilates a region to the point of dysfunction. CNS stress is moderated through varied intensity, and muscular stress is dispersed across the body. Sleep improves, soreness reduces, and readiness rebounds faster. For lifters who've struggled with joint pain, persistent soreness, or burnout under high-frequency bro splits, this recovery profile is not just beneficial—it's transformative.

There is, however, no room for ego. Full-body strength training exposes every gap. There is no hiding from weak hamstrings, poor bracing, or dysfunctional scapular movement. The frequent exposure to compound lifts shines a light on every inefficiency. But this is its greatest strength. It forces adaptation through confrontation. Progress doesn't happen in spite of flaws—it happens because the program refuses to let them persist.

Even for competitive powerlifters and weightlifters, full-body templates serve as off-season frameworks or transition phases between peaking cycles. They rebuild movement quality, address imbalances, and restore training volume after periods of high specificity. Their simplicity is deceptive. These are not beginner routines—they are structurally elegant systems that allow advanced lifters to refine execution while layering in complexity only where needed.

Ultimately, full-body training for strength is an exercise in clarity. It eliminates distraction. It aligns training frequency with neural demand. It reinforces movement over muscles and quality over quantity. It refuses to confuse exhaustion with output, or session length with effectiveness. And for lifters serious about adding weight to the bar—week after week, year after year—it offers a durable, principled model for progress.

It doesn't cater to fantasy. It doesn't glorify volume. It demands intent, attention, and patience. And in return, it delivers the only metric that strength training ever cares about: performance under the bar.

Chapter 19: Recovery Realities Across Splits

Recovery is the invisible currency of progress—earned through restraint, spent with intent, and often squandered in the name of effort. Nowhere is this more evident than in the contrasting recovery demands of the three dominant training splits: Upper/Lower, Push/Pull/Legs (PPL), and Full-Body. Each promises structure, balance, and results, but each also extracts its toll in the form of systemic and localized fatigue. The distinction between what a split demands and what the lifter can actually recover from is where most programs begin to fracture. Understanding recovery not as an afterthought but as a central design constraint is what separates a productive training plan from a slow march toward burnout.

Push/Pull/Legs presents itself as orderly, elegant, and thorough. Three clearly defined sessions, often repeated twice weekly, provide apparent frequency and coverage. Yet the six-day grind it demands often exceeds the recovery bandwidth of most natural lifters. Trained at high volume—as it typically is—PPL loads each muscle group with direct and indirect work twice per week, with minimal systemic rest. A Monday push session featuring bench press, overhead press, and triceps isolation carries over into Tuesday's pull day, where the stabilizers and scapular retractors are still fatigued. By Wednesday, legs are trained while the upper body hasn't fully recovered, and the cycle begins again with no built-in buffer. This continuous loop quietly compounds fatigue.

The central flaw in PPL recovery isn't theoretical—it's observable. Lifters start strong on Monday, maintain intensity Tuesday, and begin to slide by Thursday. Sleep becomes disrupted. Joints complain. Load stagnates. Yet because the split prescribes six days, the psychological pressure to adhere to the schedule overrides biofeedback. Instead of periodizing rest, lifters grind through cumulative fatigue, mistaking the sensation of effort for progress. What follows is a slow erosion of performance masked by volume consistency. The split hasn't failed—it's the lifter's ability to recover that's been ignored.

Upper/Lower splits, in contrast, offer a better balance between stress and recovery—particularly in four-day formats. By alternating upper and lower body sessions across the week, they naturally create localized recovery periods. Monday's upper-body effort is followed by Tuesday's lower-body focus, giving the pressing and pulling musculature 48 hours to rebound. Thursday and Friday repeat the cycle. This structure limits direct overlap and distributes systemic fatigue more manageably than PPL. Each muscle group is still trained twice weekly, but with reduced carryover stress and more strategic spacing.

Importantly, Upper/Lower splits scale more cleanly across intensity ranges. They support both hypertrophy and strength goals without forcing maximal output in back-to-back sessions. A heavy upper-body session can be followed by a lighter lower-body volume day. The lifter doesn't need to deload entire weeks—recovery modulation can be embedded in the week itself. However, this advantage is lost when lifters treat every session as a maximal event. Four days quickly becomes functionally equivalent to six when every day is a grinder. The recovery promise of Upper/Lower depends not just on structure, but on restraint.

Full-body training offers a different model entirely. It trades intra-session volume for inter-session frequency and relies on more distributed recovery to prevent overload. Muscles are trained every session, but never annihilated. This forces the lifter to reduce per-session volume and prioritize movement quality. The result is a plan where systemic fatigue is controlled by intelligent session design rather than by day-of-the-week labeling. Monday's squats don't destroy performance because they're not followed by another heavy lower-body session on Tuesday—they're followed by rest or by pressing and pulling variations performed at manageable intensity.

Because full-body training typically runs three or four days per week, it automatically includes rest days—built-in, non-negotiable recovery slots that PPL conspicuously lacks. These aren't just physical recovery opportunities; they're psychological breathers. Lifters return to training fresher, with more intent and focus. Instead of dreading the week's sixth session, they're ready to attack the third. For natural trainees— whose recovery is limited by sleep, nutrition, and life obligations—this structure isn't just beneficial. It's essential.

What's often missed in split comparison is the distinction between local and systemic fatigue. A muscle can recover in 48–72 hours. The nervous system, connective tissues, and hormonal state may need longer—especially under high loads or chronic stress. PPL's relentless pacing means that even if the target muscle is rested, the system isn't. Pressing on Monday affects deadlifts on Wednesday via thoracic fatigue, joint strain, or scapular control. Full-body and Upper/Lower plans mitigate this by rotating joint stress and emphasizing movement pattern balance. They don't eliminate fatigue—they manage it.

There's also the issue of psychological recovery. Training isn't just mechanical—it's cognitive. PPL, when run to full intensity, becomes mentally taxing. Six days of focused effort leaves little room for life stress, sleep disruption, or recovery setbacks. The lifter begins to associate training with exhaustion. Upper/Lower moderates this somewhat through variety. Full-body, again, offers the best solution by condensing effort into fewer, more focused sessions. This improves adherence not just by saving time but by preserving motivation.

Another overlooked recovery factor is joint strain accumulation. In PPL, each session focuses on a narrow set of joints repeatedly. Push days tax the elbows and shoulders. Pull days strain the biceps and lower back. Leg days load the knees and hips. Repeat this cycle twice weekly and joint irritation becomes inevitable. Upper/Lower splits reduce this repetition, and full-body training spreads joint loading across a wider array of angles and intensities. A squat one day, a lunge the next. A barbell press followed by a dumbbell variation. This reduces chronic stress and improves long-term durability.

Of course, all splits are recoverable if programmed with restraint. But lifters rarely operate under restraint. They chase volume, add exercises, and confuse soreness with stimulus. In this environment, recovery isn't just an outcome—it's a casualty. The most recoverable split is the one that forces the lifter to respect fatigue before it accumulates. Full-body training does this through structure. Upper/Lower does it through alternation. PPL, unless modified, invites overreach disguised as discipline.

The real question isn't which split recovers best in theory. It's which one recovers best in your life. If work stress cuts sleep to five hours, if diet is inconsistent, if training time is limited, PPL becomes a liability. If training four days per week with flexibility and balance is feasible, Upper/Lower excels. If consistency is possible only three days per week and recovery is at a premium, full-body wins outright.

In the end, recovery across splits isn't a matter of preference— it's a matter of cost. Every training structure incurs physiological debt. The successful plan is the one that pays it off on time, every time. Not in motivation, but in sleep quality, joint stability, consistent bar speed, and load progression. Recovery isn't optional. It's the rate-limiter on progress. And your split isn't judged by how hard you train—but by how well you can train again.

Chapter 20: Training Frequency: Truth vs Myth

Few topics in strength training inspire as much confusion— and as many half-truths—as training frequency. It is routinely overemphasized by some and willfully ignored by others, treated alternately as the holy grail of hypertrophy or a detail too minor to matter. The truth, predictably, sits somewhere between dogma and dismissal. Frequency matters—but not in the way most lifters think. It is not a standalone driver of progress. It is a variable that only becomes powerful when calibrated against volume, intensity, recovery, and progression. Without context, frequency is just noise. With it, it becomes one of the most useful tools in the programming arsenal.

The myth of frequency as magic persists because it aligns with a very human bias: the belief that doing more, more often, must deliver better results. If training a muscle twice per week is good, then surely three or four times must be great. This logic underpins many popular training models—from full-body programs to high-frequency variations of Push/Pull/Legs. But research and in-gym outcomes repeatedly show that frequency, by itself, does not increase hypertrophy if volume is held constant. A muscle group trained with 15 quality sets once per week will grow about as well as the same muscle trained with five sets across three sessions—provided those sets are matched in effort, execution, and recoverability.

This is where the first misconception collapses. Frequency is not an independent stimulus for muscle growth. It is a method of distributing volume more effectively. The real driver of hypertrophy is total weekly workload—measured not just in sets and reps, but in mechanical tension, proximity to failure, and the consistency with which that stimulus is applied. Frequency simply allows that volume to be organized in a way that reduces fatigue, improves execution, and enhances adherence. When used properly, frequency doesn't create new stimulus—it clears the runway for better stimulus to take off.

Where frequency does matter—critically—is in skill development and strength progression. Compound lifts are complex motor patterns that improve with practice. A lifter who squats twice per week will move more efficiently than one who squats once, assuming intensity is regulated. Bar path tightens, bracing becomes second nature, and rep quality increases. This doesn't just improve safety—it increases performance. A technically sound squat allows the lifter to express more force with less wasted effort, which indirectly drives hypertrophy by increasing load under tension.

The strength-specific benefit of frequency is most pronounced in natural lifters. Without pharmacological enhancement, recovery capacity is limited. Trying to compress all pressing volume into one day creates systemic fatigue that undermines later sets. Splitting that pressing volume across two sessions improves execution, maintains rep quality, and keeps the lifter fresher across each set. This logic extends to all major movement patterns. Frequency helps the lifter train harder, with better form, across more total work—without necessarily doing more work in any one session.

Another myth is the idea that high frequency automatically equates to better adherence. This is false in practice, even if it makes sense on paper. Six-day training weeks appeal to motivated beginners, but that motivation rarely survives the logistics of adult life. Miss a single day and the split collapses into confusion. By contrast, lower-frequency models—three to four sessions per week—are more resilient. Full-body and upper/lower splits succeed here because they reduce the psychological penalty of a missed workout. When each session touches the entire body or large portions of it, no muscle group is neglected, and no session is wasted. Frequency supports adherence only when it supports recovery and life compatibility.

There's also a tendency to conflate frequency with discipline. Training six days per week is seen as a badge of honor, while training three times implies laziness. This is cultural, not physiological. The body adapts to stimulus, not to schedules. There are elite powerlifters who train three days a week and set records. There are recreational lifters who train daily and make no progress. Frequency without progression is meaningless. It is not the presence of effort that matters, but the structure and sustainability of that effort over time.

In that light, frequency must be viewed as a programming dial, not a doctrine. The optimal frequency is the one that allows the lifter to hit each muscle group with sufficient volume, at sufficient intensity, with sufficient quality—and recover in time to do it again. For some, that means three full-body sessions per week. For others, it may mean a four-day upper/lower rotation. For advanced trainees with high recovery capacity, six-day PPL models can work, but only if volume is intelligently managed and recovery is prioritized. The problem arises when frequency is increased while volume and recovery remain static. This is how progress stalls, and burnout begins.

There are also diminishing returns to frequency. Beyond three exposures per week, most muscle groups don't benefit from added stimulus unless volume also increases—and even then, only if recovery is ensured. More frequent training can quickly become redundant, with overlapping fatigue and reduced training quality. There's a fine line between reinforcing a movement and overexposing it. Lifters who chase daily lifting often fail not from overtraining, but from lack of training variability and cumulative wear on connective tissues. Their frequency becomes noise—loud, exhausting, and directionless.

From a programming perspective, frequency is best used to address specific goals or weak points. A lifter with underdeveloped hamstrings may benefit from three targeted exposures per week—hip hinges on one day, leg curls on another, and glute-ham raises or RDLs elsewhere. These exposures are small—three to four sets each—but they create a cumulative stimulus without overwhelming the system. This approach is surgical. Frequency is the delivery method, not the payload. The mistake is turning frequency into the payload and expecting hypertrophy to follow automatically.

Psychologically, the right frequency reduces friction. It fits the lifter's life. It doesn't demand perfection, and it doesn't punish inconsistency. It supports momentum without becoming a burden. This is the underrated value of frequency as a behavioral tool. It keeps training accessible, especially for intermediate and advanced lifters who must balance intensity with longevity. It ensures that sessions are not so rare that technique erodes, nor so common that training becomes an obligation rather than a pursuit.

Ultimately, frequency is a framework, not a commandment. It must be adjusted in relation to all other variables: volume, intensity, recovery, and schedule. More is not better unless more can be recovered from. Less is not worse if it allows for better consistency. The goal is not to train often—it is to train well, again and again, for years. Frequency, when used wisely, helps make that possible. When used carelessly, it becomes just another way to stall out while pretending to work hard.

The truth is that frequency is neither a secret weapon nor an overrated metric. It is a lever, and like any lever, its power depends entirely on how—and when—it's pulled.

Chapter 21: Volume: The Real Driver

Volume is the heartbeat of hypertrophy. Strip away the debates about optimal splits, the endless pontificating over rest intervals, and the latest contrived "science-backed" periodization schemes, and what remains—what always remains—is volume. Not the number of hours spent in the gym, not the number of days trained per week, but the cumulative mechanical work applied to muscle fibers over time. Sets, reps, and load—executed with sufficient proximity to failure—are what actually drive muscle growth. Everything else is context or optimization. Volume is the signal. Frequency, intensity, tempo, and exercise selection are just the dials used to modulate how that signal is delivered.

The fixation on programming minutiae often obscures this truth. Lifters obsess over whether to train chest twice or three times a week, whether to use a push/pull/legs split or an upper/lower rotation, while completely ignoring whether their weekly volume is even in the effective range. The literature converges around a basic threshold: for most trained individuals, somewhere between 10 to 20 hard sets per muscle group per week constitutes a productive zone. Below this, gains stall from under-stimulation. Above it, fatigue exceeds recovery capacity, and quality collapses. This range isn't sacred—it's a reference. But what it makes clear is that training volume is not just a supporting factor. It is the foundation upon which all adaptation rests.

Volume is also where most lifters miscalculate. Beginners often think they're doing more than they are. Five movements for chest in one day may feel like high volume, but if only the first two exercises are done with true effort and the rest are glorified warm-ups, the weekly stimulus is lower than expected. Conversely, advanced lifters with high work capacity sometimes push so deep into the high-volume spectrum that recovery falters, even as sets accumulate. What matters isn't total work—it's effective work: sets taken close to failure, performed with stable mechanics and progressive load, repeated consistently across weeks.

The central mistake is mistaking duration or fatigue for volume. A two-hour workout filled with low-effort supersets, rest-pause sets done without focus, and excessive "pump work" is not high volume—it's disorganized exertion. Similarly, splitting 15 sets of back training across three sessions isn't inherently superior to doing them in two if the per-session quality drops. Volume is not just a count of sets. It is a measure of how many of those sets deliver meaningful stimulus to the muscle. When effort declines, so does the value of the set. A set is only "volume" in the hypertrophic sense if it brings muscle fibers under significant mechanical tension for sufficient time.

This is why tracking volume is not as simple as logging exercises. It requires understanding where stimulus lives in a training session. Compound movements, performed early in the session with high intent, carry more volume value than accessories done when fatigue is high and concentration low. Five sets of squats close to failure will induce more adaptation than ten casual sets of leg extensions performed half-heartedly. Not because squats are magic, but because they load the system heavily, involve multiple joints, and demand full-body engagement. Volume quality is the lever that separates productive programs from busywork.

Progressive overload is often framed as a separate concept, but in reality, it is volume's evolutionary arm. Volume must increase over time—not endlessly, but in a measured, recoverable way—to continue driving adaptation. This can be done by adding sets, reps, or load, or by improving rep quality at the same workload. The goal is not to perform more total work for its own sake but to raise the ceiling on what the muscle must adapt to. A lifter who stalls in progress often doesn't need a new split—they need a new volume ceiling, executed with focus and tracked with honesty.

The interplay between volume and recovery is where most training plans unravel. It's easy to add volume. It's harder to recover from it—especially when sleep, nutrition, and life stress aren't controlled variables. The art of programming lies in finding the edge of recoverable volume and dancing just along it without tipping over into regression. For some lifters, this might mean 14 sets per muscle group. For others, particularly older or more stressed individuals, the number might be closer to ten. It is not about finding the highest number one can survive, but the lowest number one can progress from consistently.

This is where split design must bow to volume logic. A six-day push/pull/legs routine can look impressive, but if it delivers only 8 sets per muscle group across the week because each session is abbreviated, it's volume-poor by any standard.

Conversely, a full-body routine done three times weekly might deliver 12 quality sets to each major muscle group if the right movements are chosen and executed with intent. The split is a delivery mechanism. Volume is the payload. No matter how elegant the container, if the content is underdosed, the program fails.

The idea that volume should be static is another myth that survives on repetition, not data. Lifters do not adapt linearly, and neither should their training stimulus. Volume can and should be periodized. Accumulation blocks may feature gradual volume increases—moving from 12 to 18 sets over a six-week phase—followed by deloads where total volume is slashed to facilitate recovery. This cyclical approach respects the body's adaptive curve. It provides signal when signal is needed and rest when rest is due. Lifters who stall for months often do so because they've frozen volume in place, afraid to reduce it lest they regress, but also too burned out to increase it productively.

Individual variation also plays a role. Some muscles respond better to higher volumes—particularly those with higher slow-twitch fiber content, like the quads or traps. Others, like the lower back or biceps, fatigue rapidly and recover slowly, requiring more conservative dosing. Volume allocation must be specific, not democratic. Giving every muscle the same number of sets is programmatic laziness. Target muscles need more exposure. Support muscles need enough to maintain function without interfering with bigger lifts. Full-body balance requires asymmetric programming.

The final piece is that volume must match intent. Junk volume is worse than no volume. It burns recovery without delivering progress. The lifter who throws in three more sets at the end of a session "just to be sure" often does so out of insecurity, not logic. Every set must be justified. It must contribute to a weekly target, within a pattern of overload, under conditions of sufficient recovery. If it doesn't, it isn't volume—it's noise.

Volume, then, is not just the real driver. It is the signal behind every adaptation, the metric that integrates training design, effort, recovery, and progression. It cannot be substituted, ignored, or hacked. Programs that work do so because they get volume right—both in amount and in execution. Those that don't, don't. No split, no frequency scheme, no intensity technique will ever overcome a lack of effective volume. It is not what you do once. It is what you do over and over, with increasing clarity, intent, and consistency. And that is how muscle is built.

Chapter 22: Fatigue Management: Where Splits Fail

Fatigue management is the crucible in which most training splits quietly fail. Not through catastrophic breakdowns or overt injury, but through slow, cumulative erosion of performance, motivation, and recovery. Lifters blame stagnation on programming tweaks, lack of discipline, or poor genetics, when in truth, the root cause is more structural: their split doesn't manage fatigue—it manufactures it. A poorly designed training structure can create a mismatch between stimulus and recovery so persistent that even intelligent programming within that framework eventually stalls. Fatigue is not the enemy of progress, but the mismanagement of it is.

The first place splits fail is in their denial of systemic fatigue. Push/Pull/Legs, especially in its six-day incarnation, is the worst offender. It encourages training muscles while adjacent systems remain compromised. Push day might focus on chest, shoulders, and triceps, but those same joints and connective tissues are still under strain 24 hours later when pull day asks for heavy rows and curls. Then comes leg day—often packed with deadlifts or RDLs that indirectly hammer the spinal erectors, grip, and hamstrings, just as the upper body begins to recover. By day four, the lifter has worked everything, but recovered nothing. The schedule proceeds; the system falls behind.

The fatigue isn't just local. Heavy pressing creates axial fatigue through spinal loading and bracing. Deadlifts leave the posterior chain—and nervous system—drained for days. Yet the structure of PPL doesn't account for overlapping stress. It assumes muscles recover in isolation, disconnected from joints, stabilizers, or the central nervous system. In practice, they don't. A lifter who bench presses on Monday and overhead presses on Thursday isn't giving their anterior chain four days of rest. They're asking the same tissues—rotator cuff, scapular stabilizers, triceps—to perform again before they've finished recovering from the first assault. The split doesn't fail because it's wrong in theory. It fails because it assumes ideal recovery conditions that rarely exist.

Upper/Lower splits perform better here but still have blind spots. Their advantage is simple alternation: upper-body work is followed by lower-body work, allowing at least a day for local recovery. This reduces joint strain and distributes fatigue across different systems. But it doesn't eliminate overlap. Heavy squats on Tuesday might be followed by deadlifts on Friday, with little time for the posterior chain to fully rebound. Likewise, Monday's bench press may compromise scapular function for Wednesday's rows. The structure helps—but it does not manage fatigue for you. That task still demands deliberate programming within the split: careful movement selection, load rotation, and built-in deloads.

Full-body training, often dismissed as too basic or beginner-focused, may actually be the most intelligent format for fatigue management—because it forces the lifter to consider the whole system in every session. No single muscle group can be annihilated, because every session requires output from multiple regions. This discourages junk volume and encourages exercise economy. The full-body lifter knows that hammering the quads today means dragging them into tomorrow's squats, so effort is distributed more intelligently. This structure respects the interconnected nature of fatigue. It doesn't isolate—it integrates. And that's exactly what fatigue demands.

But even full-body plans can become fatiguing if mismanaged. Too many high-intensity compound lifts, too little variation in rep ranges, or insufficient rest days can turn a three-day plan into a systemic grind. The difference is that when fatigue emerges in full-body programs, it tends to show up earlier and more clearly—through performance degradation across the board rather than in isolated movements. This makes it easier to spot, diagnose, and correct. In split routines, fatigue hides. You don't see it until progress stalls, joints ache, or sleep quality tanks.

Fatigue itself is multifactorial. There's local muscular fatigue—depletion of substrates, microtrauma, and inflammatory markers. There's neural fatigue—decline in central drive and motor unit recruitment. And there's systemic fatigue—the accumulation of hormonal, cardiovascular, and cognitive stress. Most splits only account for the first. They assume that if the muscle isn't sore, it's recovered. But neural fatigue lingers long after DOMS fades, and systemic fatigue is invisible until performance crumbles. A well-constructed training split must accommodate all three types—or at least avoid exacerbating them simultaneously.

Where splits most reliably collapse is in the middle of the week. Monday opens strong. Tuesday is still productive. By Thursday, performance drops. Volume stays high, but bar speed slows, joint discomfort emerges, and session duration balloons. The split hasn't changed—but the lifter has. Fatigue is outpacing recovery. This midweek failure isn't about motivation—it's about programming density. Training four to six days in a row compresses fatigue accumulation into a short window with no recovery outlet. The solution is not more stimulants or better time management. The solution is better split design.

Another failure point is lack of load modulation. Many splits assume every session is performed at the same intensity and volume. There's no internal wave—no light days, no submaximal sessions, no technical focus blocks. Without these, the training week becomes a series of sprints. Even if each workout is well-designed in isolation, the week as a whole becomes unsustainable. A split must not only organize muscles—it must organize fatigue. This means embedding recovery into the structure: alternating intensities, rotating rep ranges, and using session sequencing that respects cumulative load.

Accessory work is another unrecognized contributor to fatigue. Lifters cram biceps curls, triceps pushdowns, lateral raises, and abdominal work into already lengthy sessions, assuming these are low-cost movements. But volume is volume. Every additional set taxes either local recovery or systemic bandwidth. Splits fail when they treat accessory work as free volume—an error that becomes more pronounced in higher-frequency plans. Triceps trained on push day may not recover in time for Friday's overhead pressing. Hamstrings hammered after squats might still be stiff when deadlifts appear two days later. These overlaps seem minor—until they compound.

Deloads are the final frontier of fatigue management, and the place where splits reveal their true sustainability. Programs that require weekly perfection—six days on, perfect nutrition, eight hours of sleep—fall apart when reality intrudes. Work deadlines, travel, illness, or poor sleep all degrade recovery. A split that can't absorb these disruptions isn't resilient. Full-body and upper/lower formats typically adapt better, allowing a single missed session to be folded into the next week without derailing the entire plan. PPL, in contrast, becomes chaotic when disrupted. Miss pull day and you're now guessing whether to combine it with push or sacrifice it altogether. The split breaks under pressure.

The irony is that fatigue is a necessary part of training. You cannot grow or get stronger without it. But when fatigue becomes unmanageable, it ceases to be productive. It becomes noise—interfering with performance, adaptation, and motivation. Splits that fail to account for this are not just inefficient. They are unsustainable. The best split is not the one that delivers the highest effort on Monday. It's the one that allows the lifter to return Friday still strong, still moving well, and still progressing.

In the end, fatigue is the bill you pay for training. But the structure of your split determines whether that bill comes due weekly—or becomes an unpayable debt. Intelligent programming must look beyond muscle group distribution and ask harder questions: Where does this plan allow me to recover? Where does it back off? Where does it let me breathe? If your split can't answer those questions, then it isn't a training plan. It's a countdown to burnout.

Chapter 23: Lifestyle Compatibility

The best training split in the world collapses under the weight of real life. This is not a philosophical problem—it's a logistical one. Lifestyle compatibility, far more than split design or exercise selection, determines long-term adherence and outcomes. Most programs don't fail because they're scientifically flawed. They fail because they were written for imaginary people with limitless time, pristine recovery conditions, and no external obligations. A program that looks optimal on paper but can't be executed consistently is, in practice, worse than a suboptimal plan that gets done week after week without disruption. Training splits must align with how people actually live—not with how lifters wish they could train in a vacuum.

The first compatibility hurdle is time. Not just days per week, but total hours available per session. Many popular splits—particularly six-day push/pull/legs formats—assume not only daily availability but 90-minute training windows. They operate under the illusion that effort scales infinitely and that every workout is equally viable regardless of life context. But the realities of work, family, commute, and recovery aren't just background noise—they're determining constraints. A lifter with four hours per week total can't recover from the same workload as a lifter with twelve. Yet many follow the same routines, dragging themselves through overscheduled weeks while convincing themselves that perfection is non-negotiable.

Upper/Lower splits offer slightly better alignment with normal adult schedules. With a four-day structure, they allow for rest days midweek or on weekends. Sessions can be adjusted for duration—heavy and short on time-crunched days, longer on days with more flexibility. But even this requires realism. A session involving squats, Romanian deadlifts, leg presses, and accessory work isn't compatible with a 45-minute lunch break. The question is never just "Can I train four days per week?" but "Can I recover from what each of those sessions demands?" Lifestyle compatibility means designing not just around calendar availability, but around energy, sleep, and bandwidth.

Full-body routines, especially when done three days per week, align best with real-world complexity. They compress the week's essential work into fewer sessions, provide built-in recovery gaps, and reduce the psychological cost of missed workouts. If Monday is lost to a late meeting or family emergency, Wednesday still keeps the program intact. There's no need to reschedule a forgotten "arm day" or reengineer the week around missed volume. The program adapts without losing coherence. This flexibility isn't just convenient—it's what makes consistency sustainable across months and years.

But compatibility goes beyond scheduling. It extends to cognitive and emotional load. The more complicated the split, the more mental bandwidth it consumes. High-frequency, high-variation programs demand more tracking, more planning, and more decision fatigue. For some lifters, that complexity becomes an unacknowledged stressor. The idea of having to remember what variation of Romanian deadlift to perform today, which grip to use on chin-ups, and how many sets of lateral raises to superset post-pull day isn't stimulating—it's exhausting. Simpler splits reduce that overhead. They allow the lifter to show up, work hard, and leave without the session becoming a second job.

Travel and disruption are another axis of compatibility. Programs that rely on gym-specific equipment, tightly sequenced sessions, or daily attendance crumble when the lifter is away from home or off-schedule. A six-day split built around cables, machines, and exact sequencing can't be run in a garage gym or a hotel. But a three-day full-body plan built around squats, presses, rows, and lunges can. This portability doesn't just preserve training continuity—it protects psychological investment. Missing a week isn't a break in identity. It's just a shift in format.

Training splits must also accommodate recovery rhythms dictated by age, profession, and stress. A twenty-three-year-old student can survive on four hours of sleep and still bench press the next morning. A thirty-eight-year-old parent with job stress, sleep disruption, and marginal nutrition cannot. Splits

113

that assume youthful recovery rates quickly punish lifters with more constrained physiology. Here, higher frequency doesn't equal higher output—it equals faster breakdown. Programs that space volume more evenly and modulate intensity per session preserve performance better over time. They don't just ask, "Can you train today?" but "Can you perform today?"

Work schedules matter. So do social calendars. So does the non-negotiable fact that most people cannot lift six days in a row without either neglecting other obligations or faking effort. The fantasy of a perfect week—six clean meals a day, uninterrupted sleep, a fresh CNS and ideal training conditions—is incompatible with how most people live. A plan that requires all of those things to succeed is not a plan. It's fiction. The lifter who accepts this reality and chooses a split they can run at 80 percent forever will make more progress than the lifter who runs the "optimal" split at 100 percent for three weeks before abandoning it.

There's also a psychological compatibility dimension. Some lifters thrive on repetition. They prefer predictability, familiar movements, and simple session goals. For them, a three-day full-body routine built around progressive compounds offers rhythm and control. Others crave novelty. They want rotation, split complexity, and varied planes of movement. These lifters may flourish under well-structured PPL variants or upper/lower cycles with weekly variation. But the split must match the person—not the person contort themselves to the split. Forcing a minimalist through a maximalist routine, or vice versa, rarely ends in consistency.

Finally, the most insidious compatibility issue is expectation misalignment. Lifters often choose a split based on who they want to become, not who they are. A 45-hour-a-week professional picks a six-day split because that's what their favorite influencer runs. A beginner adopts an advanced upper/lower volume template because it "looks serious." These decisions are aspirational, not strategic. The result is predictable: missed sessions, inconsistent effort, skipped recovery work. The split didn't fail—the expectation did. Training plans must start from reality. Not fantasy, not future self, but current capacity. Only then can they grow with the lifter rather than collapse under them.

Lifestyle-compatible training isn't lazy or compromised. It's focused, resilient, and honest. It accounts for all of life's variables, not just those that happen inside the gym. It respects the body's capacity, the mind's limitations, and the calendar's demands. And above all, it prioritizes what actually moves the needle: showing up, doing the work, and recovering well enough to do it again. A training split is not a moral commitment. It's a functional tool. And the right one is the one that lets you keep training when life doesn't care about your macros, your mobility work, or your mesocycle.

Chapter 24: Split Adherence Rates

Training splits are rarely abandoned because they stop working. More often, they're abandoned because people stop doing them. This is not a question of effectiveness—it's a question of adherence. A program that yields 2 percent better hypertrophy gains in theory means nothing if it gets run for three inconsistent weeks, then dropped the moment work picks up or motivation falters. Adherence is the unspoken filter through which all program design must pass. If the structure doesn't fit a lifter's schedule, energy levels, and attention span, then the rest—volume, intensity, frequency—is academic. Split adherence is not just a psychological variable. It's the operational bottleneck of real-world training.

The fitness industry, enamored with optimization, often builds splits with a lab in mind, not a life. Controlled studies report training outcomes based on perfect compliance, tightly regulated conditions, and short durations. Lifters read the conclusions and adopt the plan, assuming they'll replicate the success. But in the wild, with unpredictable workweeks, family obligations, travel, poor sleep, and human inconsistency, the most elegant plan becomes an exercise in guilt management. The plan that gets done imperfectly for six months will outperform the perfect plan executed intermittently.

The adherence cliff is steepest with six-day splits, especially Push/Pull/Legs. At the start, PPL feels exciting—cleanly divided sessions, targeted focus, the illusion of hitting everything. But six days of required training per week is a fragile structure. Miss one day and the entire schedule is thrown off. Most lifters don't know how to adjust without turning the week into chaos: double up, skip, reshuffle, or restart? The result is paralysis by disruption. Motivation drops, continuity collapses, and the lifter either resets repeatedly or quietly defaults to skipping sessions altogether. What began as a methodical plan becomes a guilt spiral of inconsistency.

Studies examining adherence over time—though limited in their scope—have repeatedly shown higher compliance with three- and four-day-per-week structures. This is not surprising. Plans that demand less frequency create psychological slack.

They allow for life to intrude without programmatic collapse. A three-day full-body routine gives four off-days per week—space for missed sessions, social obligations, and mental recovery. Miss a Monday and the week still works. Miss two days and you've still hit 66 percent of your plan. The friction to re-engage is low. The plan remains intact even under stress.

Upper/Lower splits, especially the four-day variety, also show strong adherence profiles among intermediate lifters. They provide balance: two upper sessions, two lower sessions, and flexible spacing across a seven-day week. They're also easy to adjust—condensing into three days if needed by merging accessories or spacing sessions to allow for greater recovery. Importantly, they feel manageable. Each session has a clear focus but isn't overwhelming in volume. The lifter rarely feels like they've done too much or too little, which makes it easier to return session after session without burnout or second-guessing.

Adherence also suffers when splits feel redundant or uninspired. High-frequency PPL routines often become monotonous by week four. Push day is push day is push day. The same movements reappear in slightly altered sequences. When every session begins to feel like a rerun, motivation wanes—even if the results are technically sound. Full-body and upper/lower plans, by virtue of covering more muscle groups per session, introduce more movement variety. A Monday full-body session might feature squats, presses, and rows. Wednesday shifts to deadlifts, dips, and chin-ups. The variety isn't just physically stimulating—it's psychologically engaging. Consistency improves not because the lifter is more disciplined, but because the training feels more worth doing.

Adherence is further shaped by session length. If a lifter knows that today's plan will take 90 minutes minimum, they're more likely to skip it entirely when time is short. Long, high-volume sessions create an all-or-nothing dynamic: either do the whole thing or don't do it at all. This punishes partial effort and rewards avoidance. Shorter, more focused sessions—especially in full-body or minimalist upper/lower plans—create an easier psychological entry point. If the lifter knows they can train productively in 45 minutes, they're more likely to begin, which often means they'll finish. Over time, this converts into superior adherence, even if the total weekly volume is slightly lower.

Another factor in adherence is cognitive load. Complex periodization models that rotate rep ranges, intensity techniques, and exercise variations weekly may appeal to advanced trainees or coaches, but they overwhelm the average lifter. The need to check spreadsheets, remember specific RIR targets, or swap in minor lift variants can become a barrier to just training. When the plan feels like a chore to understand, it becomes easier to abandon. Adherence thrives on clarity. Knowing what today's session entails, why it matters, and how to execute it without excessive mental energy is what keeps lifters coming back—especially when life is already complicated.

Even psychological identity plays a role. Lifters who self-identify as consistent are more likely to stick with simple plans that reinforce that identity. When the plan feels doable, even on a bad day, it builds momentum. In contrast, programs that demand perfection create fragility. Miss one session and the streak is broken. Miss two and the shame spiral begins. Many high-frequency plans quietly cultivate this all-or-nothing mindset. Lifters begin to associate their program with personal failure, not physical progress. Unsurprisingly, adherence drops not because the plan stops working, but because the lifter no longer believes they can stick with it.

Perhaps the most overlooked variable in adherence is lifecycle compatibility. A split that works beautifully at age 25, during a period of minimal responsibility, may collapse entirely by 35 when careers, relationships, or children enter the picture. Yet lifters often cling to outdated templates, trying to force a six-day model into a three-day life. The solution isn't to "try harder"—it's to adapt the split. Full-body and upper/lower models excel here because they're scalable. They allow lifters to maintain training continuity even when time shrinks. This doesn't just preserve adherence—it preserves the training identity itself.

Adherence isn't solved by motivation. It's solved by structure. A split that demands six days per week punishes inconsistency. One that allows three or four days absorbs it. A plan that requires perfect conditions fails the moment real life intervenes. One that flexes with life's chaos survives. The programs lifters stick to aren't always the ones they love. They're the ones they can run without resentment, repeat without boredom, and resume without guilt. That's what makes a training split good—not its spreadsheet logic, but its real-world durability.

In the end, adherence is the metric that matters most. Because the best split is not the one that builds the most muscle in a study. It's the one a lifter can do today, tomorrow, and again next week—without breaking, stalling, or quitting. The muscles don't care what the program looks like. They only care that the work gets done. And work doesn't get done without showing up. So if a split doesn't support that—if it can't be done, lived with, and returned to—then it doesn't matter how optimal it is. It isn't yours.

Chapter 25: Psychological Fatigue and Monotony

Physical fatigue can be measured—through bar speed, heart rate, soreness, or load degradation. Psychological fatigue, by contrast, is harder to detect until it's already influencing behavior: skipped sessions, rushed workouts, or the quiet erosion of effort. Monotony, boredom, and disengagement are not signs of laziness; they're symptoms of a system that no longer stimulates. When lifters talk about burnout, they rarely mean muscular fatigue. What they're feeling is cognitive and emotional fatigue—an inability to stay mentally present in training. And this is often rooted in the structure of the training split itself.

The psychological cost of training is cumulative. A program may look balanced on paper, but if it grinds the lifter through the same motor patterns, rep ranges, and sequencing week after week, it quickly becomes cognitively deadening. The mind stops anticipating sessions with curiosity. The lifter begins to go through the motions—not because the program is physically too hard, but because it has become psychologically flat. This distinction is rarely acknowledged. A lifter who skips Friday's deadlifts isn't always tired. They're uninspired.

Push/Pull/Legs splits are especially vulnerable to this form of monotony. Their appeal lies in their compartmentalization—chest and triceps on one day, back and biceps on another, legs alone in isolation. But this same compartmentalization limits novelty. Push day becomes a fixed rotation of bench press, incline dumbbells, overhead press, and triceps extensions. Pull day follows with predictable rows and curls. After a few weeks, each session is a known quantity, not a new challenge. The lifter can recite the workout in their head before stepping into the gym. Predictability may seem like discipline, but in practice, it kills engagement.

Upper/Lower splits offer slightly more variation by distributing movement patterns across the week. Upper sessions may alternate between vertical and horizontal pressing, or include both pushing and pulling. Lower sessions can balance hinge and squat patterns, allowing more variety in sequencing. Still, even these plans can fall into psychological ruts if they lack modulation in rep schemes, load focus, or exercise rotation. The split doesn't guarantee novelty; it only creates space for it. Without conscious variation built in, the risk of mental staleness remains.

Full-body training, while often dismissed as repetitive, paradoxically offers the best framework for psychological sustainability—precisely because it requires intelligent variation. No single session can do everything, so the lifter must rotate emphasis across the week. Monday may be lower-body dominant with secondary pressing. Wednesday could emphasize pulls and carries. Friday leans into barbell work or high-tension tempo lifts. Because full-body splits are functionally limited in session length, they encourage strategic programming. Each session feels distinct—not just because the exercises change, but because the muscular and neurological demands shift.

Psychological fatigue also increases with rigid linearity. Programs that require perfect progression—add weight every week, hit one more rep each session—turn the gym into a performance test, not a training opportunity. When success is narrowly defined as beating a number, every plateau becomes a failure. This mental pressure accumulates, especially for intermediate and advanced lifters, who no longer progress linearly. They begin to associate training with anxiety or self-judgment. The irony is that these lifters aren't less motivated—they're exhausted by the constant scoreboard. A split that doesn't include variety in outcome—sessions that emphasize technique, tempo, or movement quality over sheer load—becomes a psychological trap.

Even well-designed splits can become stale if they're repeated too long without modulation. The lifter isn't overtrained—they're under-stimulated. Nothing challenges attention. No lift feels novel. The neural pathways are bored. This isn't a flaw in the lifter's mentality—it's a sign that the programming has stopped evolving. Psychological fatigue often arises not from high workload, but from low variation. The brain thrives on novelty, context-shifting, and complexity. Training that eliminates these elements, even in the name of discipline, risks disengagement.

The solution is not randomization. Randomness masquerades as variety, but it lacks coherence. What psychological fatigue demands is structured novelty—variation with purpose. Change the grip on rows. Swap the press from barbell to dumbbell. Adjust tempo or range of motion. Rotate movement families every four to six weeks while preserving core progression. Even small adjustments—moving from three sets of ten to five sets of five—can restore interest. The body responds to tension; the brain responds to difference.

Deloads and low-volume phases can also mitigate psychological fatigue. These aren't just physical recovery windows—they're mental resets. Stepping back from maximal effort, high volume, or tightly structured progressions gives the lifter a chance to train without pressure. Often, motivation returns not because the lifter rested more, but because they stopped treating every session like an exam. A week of minimalist training—three compound lifts, done without tracking—can restore engagement faster than any motivational speech.

Split design must also consider the rhythm of life. Training three days per week feels manageable for most. Four is doable with planning. Five or six quickly becomes a source of tension. Not just in the calendar, but in the psyche. A split that demands too many touchpoints per week becomes an ongoing negotiation with time, guilt, and fatigue. Psychological adherence drops not because the lifter is uncommitted, but because the plan asks for more mental real estate than it returns in satisfaction. Full-body and upper/lower splits offer more breathing room—days off, fewer decisions, reduced friction. This preserves emotional energy and reinforces identity without demanding obsession.

Even the sequencing of sessions impacts psychological load. Placing the most demanding sessions early in the week, when willpower is higher, preserves motivation. Scheduling technical or lighter sessions later in the week provides psychological relief. Alternating between strength-focused and hypertrophy-focused days shifts the lifter's frame of reference: one day is about precision, the next about pump. This interleaving of effort types keeps the brain engaged, even when the movement patterns stay familiar.

Perhaps the most overlooked source of psychological fatigue is lack of feedback. Programs that don't provide visible or felt progress leave the lifter directionless. This doesn't mean constant PRs—it means noticeable change. Improved bar speed, better form, visible pump, reduced joint pain. Splits that allow these feedback points—by including movement quality emphasis, autoregulation, or flexible progression—create small victories that compound into motivation. A program that only rewards numbers on a spreadsheet will always lose to one that delivers in-session feedback.

Monotony is not solved by motivation. It's solved by programming. The lifter who skips sessions, avoids certain lifts, or coasts through workouts is not uncommitted. They're operating under a plan that no longer stimulates the mind. And the fix isn't to grind harder—it's to program smarter. Psychological fatigue is real, measurable in its effects, and preventable through better design.

A split that manages this well becomes more than a plan—it becomes a sustainable practice. It respects the lifter's physiology, yes, but also their cognition, emotions, and rhythm of engagement. Because progress isn't just about adding more weight. It's about showing up with purpose. And purpose cannot survive monotony. It needs variety, feedback, and structure that feels alive. Without that, even the most effective split becomes a prison. With it, the same split becomes a framework for years of consistent, focused, satisfying work.

Chapter 26: Beginners vs Intermediates vs Advanced

Training splits are often prescribed with a tone of finality—do this program, follow this template, repeat for results. Yet the effectiveness of any split depends entirely on who is running it. A training plan that serves a beginner well may stall an intermediate, and a structure that sustains advanced lifters may crush someone with only six months of experience. Progression in training isn't just about lifting heavier weights—it's about adapting your training structure to match your capability, recovery, and goals at each stage. Splits are not one-size-fits-all. They are tools that must scale, and most don't.

For beginners, the primary need is exposure—exposure to movement patterns, to consistent training rhythm, and to basic progression models. Complexity is not only unnecessary at this stage; it's counterproductive. The body is hyper-responsive to stimulus in the early months of training. Neuromuscular efficiency improves session to session. Gains arrive almost regardless of split—as long as the work gets done. What the beginner needs most is practice: frequent exposure to squats, presses, pulls, and hinges, performed with reasonable load and close attention to form. Full-body training, three days per week, is unrivaled in its efficiency here. It provides high frequency without high fatigue, maximizes skill acquisition, and simplifies the weekly structure.

The fatal error most beginners make is copying the splits used by their favorite influencers—six-day bro-splits, PPL rotations with isolated arm days, or upper/lower plans saturated with accessory work. These plans assume a base level of work capacity, connective tissue conditioning, and motor control that beginners do not have. The result is fatigue without mastery. The lifter gets sore, not strong. They confuse complexity for progress. Worse, they often skip the foundational movements entirely in favor of pump-driven isolation work. The body adapts quickly at first—but to what? Poor technique, underloaded compound lifts, and an overreliance on machines. Six months later, the same lifter is still repping out cable flies with no meaningful load progression.

Intermediates face a different challenge. At this stage, the low-hanging fruit is gone. Technique has solidified, the bar no longer moves faster each week, and the margin for error in recovery and intensity begins to narrow. Volume must rise. Progression becomes more deliberate. This is when split structure starts to matter—not because it drives adaptation directly, but because it organizes workload in a way that supports increasing training demands. Full-body work still has value here, but many intermediates benefit from moving to a four-day upper/lower split. It allows for slightly more volume per muscle group, increased training density, and more focused loading strategies.

Upper/lower splits also begin to introduce intelligent fatigue management. Heavy squats no longer share the same session as heavy pressing. Hinge and squat patterns can be separated by several days. Muscle groups receive adequate stimulus twice per week without the overlap fatigue seen in high-frequency full-body work. Importantly, these splits allow for autoregulation: a lower-body day can be emphasized or dialed back depending on recovery. The intermediate lifter is now managing resources, not just pushing effort. They are beginning to train like an athlete, not a gym enthusiast.

PPL splits also enter the conversation at the intermediate stage, though with a critical caveat: few intermediates can recover from six hard sessions per week. The common mistake is adopting a PPL template without modulating volume or intensity. Every push day becomes a 20-set chest annihilation. Pull day is a grip-taxing marathon. Legs get buried under squats, RDLs, lunges, and machine work—all in one session. The system drowns in accumulated fatigue. The structure works—but only if sessions are trimmed, rest is respected, and recovery capacity is matched to output. A modified PPL run five days per week—rotating through the sequence with rest days as needed—is often a better fit.

For advanced lifters, structure becomes even more critical—but paradoxically, less rigid. These lifters have earned the right to break rules because they understand the consequences. They can run an upper/lower split that blends in PPL sequencing. They can rotate weekly emphases—one week hypertrophy dominant, the next intensity focused. They understand how to sequence movement patterns to avoid redundant stress, how to manage volume waves, and how to rotate assistance lifts without derailing core lifts. In short, they can build their own split within the framework of intelligent training.

But even advanced lifters must respect recovery. High-volume PPL or body-part splits only work for those who've built the capacity to recover from them—and even then, only when life allows. Many advanced lifters, particularly those not using performance-enhancing drugs, benefit from returning to more minimalistic structures: three- to four-day plans with focused intensity, built-in rest, and minimal accessory fluff. What changes isn't the structure—it's the quality of work inside it. An advanced lifter can generate more stimulus with five sets than a beginner can with fifteen. The split doesn't need to expand—it needs to concentrate.

Another layer of complexity for advanced lifters is specificity. Beginners and intermediates grow from general exposure. Advanced lifters grow from precision. Their split must reflect their goals: strength, hypertrophy, power, or athletic performance. A powerlifter's week may center around three lifts and rotate accessories accordingly. A physique athlete may need high-frequency exposure to lagging body parts, requiring careful sequencing to avoid overtraining. Here, split structure becomes a delivery system for specific adaptations. The advanced lifter no longer asks, "Which split should I follow?" but "Which split delivers what I'm trying to build?"

Across all stages, the danger is mismatch—using a split suited to a different level of development. Beginners overwhelmed by complexity. Intermediates stagnating under minimalism. Advanced lifters burned out by overly ambitious frequency. The structure must match the system it's applied to. A split isn't good or bad in isolation—it's good or bad relative to the lifter's context. Age, training age, work capacity, recovery rate, and life constraints all dictate what can be sustained.

The irony is that the split most lifters need is rarely the one they want. Beginners crave complexity. Intermediates want to train like pros. Advanced lifters often long for the simplicity of beginner gains. But chasing the wrong structure at the wrong time doesn't accelerate progress—it derails it. Progress in training isn't just about more—it's about better: better stimulus, better recovery, better sequencing. And that only happens when the split evolves with the lifter, not ahead of them.

In the end, the best split is the one that matches the lifter's stage—not aspirationally, but functionally. It doesn't just distribute volume. It distributes focus. It creates space for effort and room for recovery. And above all, it respects the single most important rule of training progression: do what works for where you are—not where you wish you were.

Chapter 27: Periodizing Across Splits

Periodization is often misrepresented as a rigid sequencing of hypertrophy, strength, and deload phases tied neatly into color-coded calendars. But in reality, periodization is simply the structured manipulation of training variables over time to sustain progress. For lifters who train long enough, this inevitably means more than changing rep ranges or load schemes—it means moving between different training splits entirely. Just as muscles need variation in stimulus, the training structure itself must sometimes evolve to avoid stagnation, address new goals, or reflect changes in lifestyle and recovery. Periodizing across splits is not program hopping. It is a deliberate recalibration of training architecture to match the shifting demands of adaptation.

Most lifters treat their chosen split like a permanent home. They settle into a Push/Pull/Legs rotation or an upper/lower template and resist any deviation, even when progress stalls or life changes. But no split is universally optimal. Each has strengths and blind spots that emerge more clearly as a lifter progresses. Staying with one format indefinitely is a recipe for diminishing returns. Periodizing across splits allows the lifter to rotate structural emphasis—moving from high-frequency to high-intensity phases, from broad exposure to focused refinement, or from volume accumulation to recovery-driven recalibration.

The key is timing. Transitions between splits should not be driven by boredom, fatigue, or social media trends. They should be dictated by the need to change how stimulus is organized. Consider the lifter who has spent 12 weeks on a hypertrophy-focused PPL split. Volume is high, frequency sits at five to six sessions per week, and most muscles are trained twice in seven days. At some point, the body stops responding—not because the exercises stopped working, but because the nervous system, connective tissue, and recovery capacity can no longer keep pace. Rather than force-feed more volume or switch to a "shock" program, the intelligent move is to shift to a lower-frequency split—perhaps an upper/lower or full-body plan that prioritizes load and rep quality over set quantity.

This shift isn't a reset. It's a new phase in the same overarching progression. The lifter maintains key movement patterns— squat, hinge, press, row—but changes how they're distributed across the week. Volume drops, but intensity may rise. Total weekly fatigue is reduced, allowing the lifter to recover while still progressing on foundational lifts. After four to six weeks in this lower-frequency model, the lifter can reintroduce volume gradually, now within a split that better reflects current capacity. The principle remains the same: adaptation plateaus are not always solved by new exercises. Sometimes, they're solved by new structures.

Another scenario emerges when transitioning from strength-focused blocks to hypertrophy-driven training. Many lifters spend extended periods in low-rep, high-load zones—often organized in full-body or upper/lower splits tailored to powerlifting. These programs develop neurological efficiency but accumulate systemic fatigue and reduce per-session volume. When the goal shifts to muscle growth, simply adding more reps or sets to the same split doesn't work. The recovery architecture is mismatched. Instead, moving to a hypertrophy-oriented split—PPL, modified bro-split, or high-frequency full-body—allows for higher volumes per muscle group, greater exercise variety, and less axial loading.

Crucially, the change in split also changes mental engagement. Different sessions feel fresh not just in content, but in structure. A lifter moving from a powerlifting-style full-body program to a targeted hypertrophy split experiences shorter rest periods, more pump work, and a return to muscular fatigue. The nervous system gets a break. Local fatigue becomes the training driver again. These transitions are not arbitrary—they are recovery tactics dressed as programming variation.

Even deloads benefit from structural periodization. Most lifters treat deloads as reduced volume within the same split. But this often fails to create true recovery. The lifter still trains six days a week, still executes the same movement patterns, and still commits the same mental effort—just with lighter loads or fewer sets. A more effective approach is to switch to a radically different split, even temporarily. For example, after a dense PPL mesocycle, a week of full-body training on non-consecutive days with minimalist compound lifts provides both muscular rest and neural recalibration. The change in frequency, duration, and exercise selection enhances recovery without abandoning the training habit.

Periodizing across splits also addresses life stages. A four-day upper/lower plan may be ideal during a stable work period, but during travel or increased work stress, a three-day full-body split ensures consistency. When life calms down, the lifter can phase back into a higher-frequency model. The goal is to keep the lifter training with intent, not grinding through sessions that no longer fit the context. Structured transitions ensure that the lifter doesn't just train more or less—they train differently, in ways that preserve stimulus while adjusting load, effort, and mental strain.

Hybrid approaches can also serve as transitional tools. A lifter finishing a PPL cycle might shift to a rotating upper/lower/PPL format—training four days weekly, but varying the split week to week. One week might include push, pull, upper, and lower; the next might repeat the cycle with different emphases. These transitions smooth the jump between distinct programs, reduce monotony, and allow experimentation with recovery strategies. They also help advanced lifters explore new structures without abandoning the progression logic built over months of training.

The mistake lifters make when shifting splits is throwing out the entire system. Exercises are changed, volume reset, loading protocols discarded. Progression gets lost. Periodization across splits should preserve continuity where possible—keeping primary lifts in place, tracking performance over time, and shifting only the delivery system. If a lifter has added 20 pounds to their Romanian deadlift during a PPL block, they should continue progressing that lift in their next split, even if the frequency or context changes. Structural variation without progression continuity is novelty without purpose.

These transitions also prevent psychological burnout. Training doesn't just fatigue the body—it fatigues the mind. Six weeks of grinding heavy triples take a toll, just as endless pump-driven hypertrophy work creates mental fatigue through repetition and redundancy. Shifting splits periodically refreshes motivation, not through arbitrary change, but by altering stimulus pathways. New movement combinations, session formats, and recovery rhythms create renewed attentiveness. This is not entertainment programming—it's engagement maintenance. Lifters who never change splits often don't notice they've stopped training with intent. Periodization across splits wakes them up.

The timeline for these transitions isn't fixed. Some lifters can run a given split for 12 to 16 weeks before diminishing returns. Others benefit from shorter cycles—six to eight weeks of focused training, then a structural shift. What matters is the recognition of fatigue, stagnation, or lifestyle friction. When progress slows, when soreness accumulates without performance gains, or when motivation drops, the split—not just the program—may be the problem. Reorganizing training to distribute stress differently is not defeat. It's how longevity in lifting is sustained.

In the end, periodizing across splits is not about novelty. It's about function. It's a strategic reshuffling of training variables to preserve intensity, manage fatigue, and maintain psychological engagement. The goal isn't to find the perfect split. The goal is to cycle intelligently through useful ones, in service of long-term progression. Because training is not a static pursuit. It evolves. And the lifter who evolves with it—through structured, deliberate transitions—will outlast, outperform, and outgrow those who cling to a single split, long after it stops delivering.

Chapter 28: Hybrid Programs and Frankenstein Routines

Hybrid programs appeal to the ambitious and the indecisive in equal measure. On paper, they promise the best of all worlds: high-frequency muscle exposure, strategic volume distribution, intensity cycling, novelty, and lifestyle flexibility. In reality, most hybrid programs devolve into Frankenstein routines—stitched-together fragments of other plans, none of which were designed to coexist. A push/pull/legs rotation, fused with an upper/lower template, crossbred with full-body weekends and an arm day thrown in "just to cover everything." It sounds clever. It often looks impressive. And it rarely works for long.

At their core, hybrid routines aim to solve legitimate problems. Lifters want frequency but also recovery. They want intensity without burnout. They crave variety without chaos. The rigidity of classic splits doesn't always fit life, especially for intermediates and advanced trainees navigating shifting work schedules, inconsistent energy, or multiple training goals. The intention behind hybrids is logical: blend the benefits of different splits to create something more sustainable or more stimulating. But intention is not structure. Without an organizing principle, hybrid programs become incoherent—volume is misallocated, fatigue isn't managed, and progression gets lost in the shuffle.

The first red flag of a Frankenstein routine is inconsistency in training frequency. One week features six sessions. The next has three. Some weeks hit muscle groups twice, others once. This erratic exposure disrupts adaptation. The body thrives on predictable stimulus-response cycles. If the chest is trained with high volume on Monday and then again randomly on Saturday—but skipped the following week entirely—the recovery signals become confused. Progress stalls not from undertraining or overtraining, but from inconsistent signaling. Muscles adapt to what they can expect. Hybrid routines that constantly shift emphasis don't allow this expectation to form.

Another common flaw is the misuse of muscle group prioritization. In an effort to "hit everything," lifters often double-count certain muscles—pressing on push day, again on upper day, again in a full-body workout with dips or dumbbell presses. The shoulders and triceps get obliterated multiple times per week, while other muscle groups—often posterior chain or hamstrings—are forgotten or under-trained. The result is both fatigue imbalance and developmental asymmetry. The hybrid program hasn't achieved higher efficiency. It's simply redistributed chaos.

Volume tracking becomes another casualty. Traditional splits make volume easy to calculate—if you train back twice per week and perform four exercises per session, you can approximate total sets. In hybrids, volume is scattered across overlapping days. Is a chin-up on upper day part of back volume or biceps volume? Does an overhead press on full-body day count toward push totals or shoulder-specific work? Without clear boundaries, tracking becomes guesswork. And once volume becomes an estimate, overload becomes an accident.

Progression—arguably the spine of any meaningful program—often vanishes entirely in Frankenstein routines. Each day is built around a different focus, but with no clear progression model across weeks. A Monday deadlift might jump from 3x5 to 4x6 with no rationale. An incline bench rotates in and out without consistent loading. Accessories change based on mood. There's no baseline, no trajectory—just movement for the sake of movement. The lifter may feel busy, sore, and accomplished, but they're drifting. Muscle is built through consistent overload, not creative choreography.

And yet, hybrid structures can work—when they're built intentionally. The difference lies in hierarchy. A good hybrid program establishes clear priorities. It defines which movement patterns or muscle groups receive primary focus, which get secondary support, and which are simply maintained. For example, a lifter running a modified upper/lower/PPL hybrid might decide that this training block prioritizes quads and back. Monday's lower session begins with heavy squats. Thursday's pull session emphasizes rows and chins. Other days—pressing, arms, accessories—support but don't dominate. Volume is allocated accordingly. Recovery is planned. The split is hybrid in structure, but focused in purpose.

Frequency must also be managed with symmetry and sustainability. Hitting legs Monday, again on Thursday, and then tacking on barbell lunges Saturday might feel productive, but without programmed variation in load, tempo, or exercise selection, the week becomes a cycle of accumulating fatigue. A proper hybrid program varies intensity across sessions: heavy bilateral squats on one day, lighter unilateral work on another. The goal is not to train more, but to train smarter across multiple exposures.

Autoregulation can also play a role. Advanced lifters often benefit from having multiple frameworks on hand—a PPL baseline, with upper/lower variants to substitute when time is short or fatigue is high. This hybrid model adapts to life without derailing progression. But the key is constraint. You can't substitute randomly. You need predefined templates: if push day can't happen, it defaults to an upper-body session that still maintains core lifts. This flexibility supports consistency. It doesn't encourage improvisation.

Hybrid plans also demand more precise recovery strategies. It's easy to overreach when combining splits. Heavy pulls Monday, squats Wednesday, and RDLs Friday sound fine until you realize the erectors, glutes, and grip are under non-stop load. A well-designed hybrid adjusts these placements. Pulls are spread out. Movement types alternate: vertical one day, horizontal the next. Deloads are built in not just by dropping volume, but by changing structure—three full-body sessions one week instead of five split sessions to allow full-system recalibration.

Psychological engagement is often cited as a reason to hybridize, but novelty cannot replace structure. A program should be engaging, but it should also be coherent. Too many lifters assemble their routines like a buffet—picking a little of everything, based on mood or media influence. What results is a plan with no logic, no progression, and no identity. It's exciting until it isn't. Then it becomes noise. A hybrid must have a spine. Not every session needs to look the same, but every session must fit into a broader architecture. You are not programming for stimulation. You are programming for adaptation.

The temptation to hybridize is strong. It offers the illusion of mastery—the idea that you've outgrown rigid templates and can now construct your own path. But freedom without structure is just disorder. True hybrid programming isn't about freedom. It's about integration. It asks: can I take two or more proven frameworks and blend them into something more tailored, more sustainable, and more precise? If the answer is yes, then the result isn't a Frankenstein routine. It's a mature system—built with foresight, run with discipline, and adaptable without collapse.

But if the answer is no—if you're blending out of boredom, ego, or confusion—then what you've created isn't innovative. It's incoherent. And incoherence doesn't build muscle, strength, or resilience. It builds fatigue, inconsistency, and stagnation, hidden under the illusion of variety.

A hybrid plan should clarify your training, not clutter it. It should simplify decision-making, not complicate it. And most of all, it should progress—week to week, block to block, across seasons of life. If it can't do that, it doesn't matter how many clever split formats it merges. It's just decoration. And muscle is not built on decoration. It's built on structure.

Chapter 29: Split Myths That Refuse to Die

Some training myths fade with time. Others dig in, adapt, and evolve—becoming harder to dislodge because they offer simple answers in a world of conditional truths. The world of training splits is particularly vulnerable to these myths, not because the splits themselves are flawed, but because they've been wrapped in half-truths, dogma, and nostalgia. Lifters cling to these ideas because they're convenient, familiar, and usually delivered with the confidence of someone who looks the part. But a myth repeated by someone with big arms is still a myth. And in the case of split routines, several continue to persist long after they should've been retired.

The first and most persistent: that more training days equals more gains. This is the myth that fuels the cult of the six-day PPL cycle and the fetishization of frequency. It's not hard to see where it comes from. More sessions seem to imply more volume, and more volume, as every lifter knows, is a primary driver of hypertrophy. But the logic breaks down under scrutiny. Volume is not the same as frequency, and adding training days without adjusting for quality, intensity, and recovery only increases junk volume and systemic fatigue. Six mediocre workouts do not outperform three focused, progressive ones. In many cases, they underperform—because fatigue accumulates faster than adaptation. Frequency is a tool, not a scoreboard.

Another enduring myth is the superiority of body-part splits for hypertrophy. The so-called "bro-split"—chest on Monday, back on Tuesday, legs on Wednesday—has been the default for decades, especially in physique circles. The appeal is intuitive: train a single muscle group per day, destroy it with volume, and let it recover for a week. It sounds efficient. In reality, it's not. Hypertrophy responds better to multiple exposures per week, not single bouts followed by six days of neglect. Hitting a muscle twice with moderate volume yields more consistent protein synthesis than annihilating it once. Elite bodybuilders get away with body-part splits because they have the pharmacological assistance to recover from that much trauma. Drug-free lifters usually just get sore.

Then there's the myth that full-body training is only for beginners. This idea persists because full-body splits are simple—and simplicity is often mistaken for inferiority. But simplicity is not the same as inefficiency. In fact, for many lifters with real-world time constraints, full-body training is the most efficient way to apply meaningful stimulus across the entire body with limited sessions. It forces prioritization, discourages fluff, and increases frequency without excessive fatigue. Olympic lifters and many seasoned strength athletes use full-body templates well into advanced stages of development—not because they can't handle more complexity, but because they know what works. The notion that you "graduate" from full-body training is fiction invented by people who mistake complexity for progress.

Closely related is the belief that certain splits are for certain goals—PPL for hypertrophy, full-body for fat loss, upper/lower for strength. These classifications are tidy, but inaccurate. Every split can be tailored for any goal. Hypertrophy is about volume and mechanical tension. Strength is about load and specificity. Fat loss is primarily diet. The split simply organizes effort. A full-body plan can build mass if it includes enough weekly volume. A PPL split can build strength if compound lifts are prioritized and intensity is managed. Rigidly assigning goals to splits is like assigning personalities to tools. A hammer isn't "aggressive." It just needs the right job.

There's also the idea that muscle confusion is necessary for growth—a myth that fuels constant program hopping and Frankenstein splits. Lifters rotate from PPL to upper/lower to full-body every two weeks, convinced that change alone is what keeps progress alive. But adaptation doesn't come from confusion—it comes from progression. The body needs repeated stimulus to create overload. Variation has its place, but it must be structured. New exercises without progression are entertainment, not training. The best split is one that allows you to track performance over time. Confusion, especially when unstructured, simply resets the adaptation clock.

Another seductive half-truth is that soreness is an indicator of effectiveness. This is deeply ingrained in split culture—particularly among those running high-volume body-part days. The goal becomes destruction, not progression. If you're not sore the next day, did you even train? But soreness is a poor metric. It often reflects novelty, not intensity. A new movement or rep range can leave you wrecked, even if the session did nothing for long-term adaptation. Some of the most effective training blocks are the ones that produce minimal soreness—because the body is adapted, recovered, and performing efficiently. The obsession with post-workout pain leads lifters to chase inflammation rather than growth.

Equally misguided is the belief that every muscle group must be trained equally in each split. Many programs, especially those copied from general templates, assign symmetrical volume across all muscle groups regardless of individual need. But the human body isn't symmetrical in development or recovery. A lifter with underdeveloped hamstrings and an overdeveloped chest should not run a textbook upper/lower split with equal load. The split must reflect personal imbalances, not just training tradition. Sticking rigidly to "balanced" splits can reinforce asymmetries or stall progress by failing to prioritize what matters.

One of the more recent myths, shaped by influencer culture, is that aesthetics require isolation, and function requires compounds. The implication is that a hypertrophy-focused PPL must be saturated with lateral raises, cable flyes, and triceps pushdowns, while a "functional" split demands sled pushes and Turkish get-ups. But this dichotomy is false. Aesthetics and function are not mutually exclusive. Compounds build aesthetics. Isolation movements can enhance function when used strategically. The split doesn't define the outcome—the exercise selection, load, and progression do. Marrying aesthetic goals with functional strength is not about choosing the right split. It's about applying the right tools, regardless of split format.

Perhaps the most paralyzing myth of all is that there is one optimal split. Lifters waste months searching for the "perfect" program structure, convinced that a 10 percent improvement in theoretical efficiency will unlock stalled progress. But training isn't a math problem with one correct answer. It's a process of adaptation under constraint. The optimal split is the one you can run consistently, recover from, and progress within. For some, that's three days a week full-body. For others, it's five days of upper/lower. For a rare few, it's a textbook PPL. The pursuit of the optimal split often masks a refusal to confront what actually limits progress: inconsistency, poor nutrition, lack of sleep, or misplaced effort.

Myths persist not because they're convincing, but because they're comforting. They simplify choices, reduce uncertainty, and offer the illusion of mastery. But in training, as in biology, the truth is rarely neat. Progress depends on precision, not dogma. And the lifter who breaks from myth—who chooses structure based on need, not narrative—is the one who grows. Splits are tools. Myths are stories. If you want results, put down the storybook and pick up the wrench.

Chapter 30: Split Decision: The Final Word

There is no single best training split, and anyone claiming otherwise is either selling something or projecting their own context onto yours. The obsession with finding the "right" split—whether it's full-body, upper/lower, or push/pull/legs—is a distraction from the more critical questions: How often can you train? How well do you recover? What lifts do you need to progress? And most importantly, what structure allows you to do that consistently over time without burning out, breaking down, or becoming bored? The final word on training splits is not a verdict. It's a framework: structured enough to guide, flexible enough to adapt.

Most lifters search for the ideal split as though it's a secret code they've failed to crack. But splits are not magical. They're just systems for organizing volume, intensity, frequency, and recovery. The same lifter can thrive under multiple splits across different phases of life or training goals. What matters isn't which split you start with—it's whether you can sustain effort within it, recover adequately between sessions, and progress in key movement patterns. Those are the pillars. The rest is window dressing.

Each split exists because it solves a problem for a particular context. Full-body training condenses effective volume into three to four weekly sessions, maximizing efficiency and reducing complexity. It suits beginners, busy professionals, and advanced lifters entering a recovery phase. It encourages frequency, skill development, and whole-body fatigue distribution. But it also requires attention to session design—because with only three exposures per week, exercise selection and load matter more, not less. Done well, full-body training delivers remarkable returns with minimal time investment. Done poorly, it becomes a random circuit that never progresses.

Upper/lower splits strike a balance between focus and frequency. Four sessions per week allow muscles to be trained twice, with enough space between exposures to recover, particularly for compound lifts. These splits excel for intermediate lifters building toward more volume but still needing recovery space between sessions. They also suit lifters who prefer clear muscle group divisions without the extreme compartmentalization of a bro-split. Upper/lower splits require strategic variation in intensity—loading heavy squats and presses on the same week demands intelligent planning to avoid system-wide fatigue. But their rhythm is intuitive, and their flexibility makes them sustainable long-term.

Push/pull/legs thrives in volume-driven hypertrophy environments. It allows a lifter to train each muscle group with high specificity and frequency—if, and only if, recovery is available to match the output. Six-day PPL routines are seductive because they feel productive: always training, always moving. But for most lifters, the cumulative fatigue outpaces the adaptation curve. Sessions become rushed or diluted. Recovery suffers. What began as a hyper-productive structure morphs into a fatigue trap. A properly run PPL requires as much discipline in rest as in effort—rotating emphasis, managing volume, and knowing when to pull back. The split isn't flawed. It's just often misapplied.

Every split has a lifecycle. What works in one training phase may overstay its welcome in the next. The smart lifter evolves their split the same way they evolve their loading schemes or exercise selection. Periodizing across splits allows for recovery, renewed stimulus, and psychological re-engagement. After 12 weeks of high-frequency training, a shift to a lower-frequency upper/lower plan can allow intensity to rise while total fatigue drops. A full-body phase might follow a dense hypertrophy block, giving joints a break and re-centering attention on bar speed, tempo, or movement quality. Splits are not identities. They are seasons. Knowing when to rotate is what separates consistency from burnout.

It is also critical to match your split to your actual life—not your ideal one. Many lifters plan around the best-case scenario: six days available, perfect recovery, immaculate motivation. But training doesn't happen in a vacuum. Work, stress, sleep, and energy are real variables. A split that assumes your life won't interrupt your schedule is already flawed. The most effective split is the one that continues working when life gets messy. It doesn't just fit into your calendar—it survives it. A three-day full-body routine that always gets done will beat a five-day PPL that's always half-finished.

Recovery isn't a luxury—it's the engine of adaptation. The best split in the world collapses if recovery can't keep up. This isn't just about sleep and food—it's about fatigue management inside the week. Do your sessions compete with each other, or complement each other? Does your lower body day leave your posterior chain fried for three days, just in time for deadlifts? Are your pressing sessions spaced to actually recover from the one before? Good split design manages internal competition. It doesn't just stack sessions like Tetris blocks—it sequences them to let the lifter keep lifting.

Split design must also respect psychological bandwidth. Many lifters fail not from lack of effort, but from program fatigue. Overly complicated splits create decision fatigue. Overly rigid ones become a burden when life changes. The best splits are cognitively frictionless: you know what day it is, what you're training, and why it matters. You don't need to check spreadsheets or scroll old notes just to figure out if today is push or pull. Good design reduces thinking. It allows effort to rise because complexity stays low.

In the end, all splits are compromises. Full-body trades session length for frequency. Upper/lower trades total volume for simplicity. PPL trades recovery for specificity. There is no perfect plan. Only better matches to your current training age, goals, schedule, and tolerance. The lifter who understands this stops chasing optimization and starts chasing progression. Because no matter how beautifully structured a split is, it's still just a container. It's what you put inside—the lifts, the effort, the progression—that determines results.

Split decision is not a one-time choice. It's a recurring evaluation. You assess what's working, what's stalling, what your body's telling you, and what your life can support. Then you adapt. Not reactively, but strategically. You don't wait until you're overtrained, demotivated, or stalled. You observe, adjust, and transition with purpose. That's the difference between a lifter who trains for three months and one who trains for thirty years.

So the final word is not a declaration of superiority. It's a call to precision. Know what you're trying to build. Understand what your life can support. Select a structure that channels effort, not one that fragments it. Then run it hard, long enough to adapt, and be honest enough to change when it stops working. The muscles don't care what split you use. They care that you train, recover, and repeat—week after week, block after block, year after year. Choose the split that lets you do that. Then get to work.

Disclaimer

The information in this book is provided for educational and informational purposes only and is not intended as medical advice. Neither the author nor Southerland Publishing is a medical professional. You should always consult a qualified health care provider before beginning any new diet, exercise program, supplement regimen, or treatment plan. Reliance on any content in this book is solely at your own risk. Southerland Publishing and the author disclaim all liability for any injuries, losses, or damages that may arise from the use or misuse of the information contained herein. Seek personalized guidance from a licensed practitioner for your unique health needs.

Made in the USA
Monee, IL
05 July 2025

20558711R00085